Penguin Education

Penguin Modern Economics Texts
General Editor: B. J. McCormick

Development Economics
Editor: Peter Robson

Land Reform and Economic Development
Peter Dorner

Peter Dorner

Land Reform and
Economic Development

Penguin Books

Penguin Books Ltd, Harmondsworth,
Middlesex, England
Penguin Books Inc, 7110 Ambassador Road,
Baltimore, Md 21207, USA
Penguin Books Australia Ltd,
Ringwood, Victoria, Australia

First published 1972
Copyright © Peter Dorner, 1972

Made and printed in Great Britain by
C. Nicholls & Company Ltd,
Set in Monotype Times

Penguin Modern Economics Texts

This volume is one in a series of unit texts designed to reduce the price of knowledge for students of economics in universities and colleges of higher education. The units may be used singly or in combination with other units to form attractive and unusual teaching programmes. The volumes will cover the major teaching areas but they will differ from conventional books in their attempt to chart and explore new directions in economic thinking. The traditional divisions of theory and applied, of positive and normative and of micro and macro will tend to be blurred as authors impose new and arresting ideas on the traditional corpus of economics. Some units will fall into conventional patterns of thought but many will transgress established beliefs.

Penguin Modern Economics Texts are published in units in order to achieve certain objectives. First, a large range of short texts at inexpensive prices gives the teacher flexibility in planning his course and recommending texts for it. Secondly, the pace at which important new work is published requires the project to be adaptable. Our plan allows a unit to be revised or a fresh unit to be added with maximum speed and minimal cost to the reader.

The international range of authorship will, it is hoped, bring out the richness and diversity in economic analysis and thinking.

B.J.McC.

To Lois

Contents

15
38

Editorial Foreword

Development economics is one of the newer branches of economics whose subject matter is the explanation of underdevelopment and measures to overcome it. Viewed in this light it is essentially a part of political economy in which political, social and institutional considerations are not neglected.

There is a case for the view that Adam Smith was the first development economist. But although current interest in the subject has rightly directed attention to neglected 'development aspects' of the thought of prominent nineteenth and early twentieth century economists, the interests of these writers and of their successors who wrote in the early part of the twentieth century lay for the most part elsewhere. Certainly few of the latter were centrally interested in growth and hardly any in underdevelopment. In this respect the situation has undergone a marked change in the last twenty years. During this period there has been a widespread and growing concern with the problems of the poorer three quarters of the earth. Academic interest has reflected this concern and in the outcome, development economics has emerged as a distinct area of study.

Land reform in a narrow sense refers to measures to redistribute land in favour of peasants and small farmers. More broadly it may be taken to embrace consolidation and registration in areas where customary tenure is prevalent and also land settlement on new lands. Land reform is obviously not a modern phenomenon. In its traditional sense, it has taken place over the years primarily in response to the demand for greater equality or social justice. Although this continues to be an important aspect of a number of contemporary land reforms, what is new is the attention which is now being given to its developmental implications, and to its possible contribution to improved agricultural productivity and expanded employment. Land reform alone, however, is unlikely to achieve much. If it is to contribute significantly to these objectives, it will clearly be necessary for it to be undertaken in conjunction with a variety of supporting institutional improvements including better credit provision, marketing facilities and extension and advisory services.

In this book the author first discusses the relationship between land reform and economic development and the diversity of existing tenure systems in different parts of the world. He goes on to consider the ways in which different countries have dealt with the acquisition of land and the post-reform tenure systems which have been adopted. In the light of this background, the following chapters evaluate land reform measures in terms of several developmental aspects, namely changes in distribution and their economic implications, and changes in employment and productivity.

Professor Dorner has had extensive first hand experience of land reform in Latin America. More recently as a member of the FAO Special Committee on Land Reform, he has obtained further experience of the issues in the rather different contexts of Asia, the Middle East and Latin America. His position as Director of the Land Tenure Research Center at the University of Wisconsin has placed him in a uniquely informed position in relation to land reform questions. In this book he makes a constructive addition to the literature, bringing to bear on a field in which general surveys are few, a wide knowledge of land tenure forms and reforms, their purposes and achievements. His contribution provides a balanced appraisal of the issues, alternatives and experience in a policy area in which many important experiments are in progress today and others are surely in prospect.

Preface

As with most fundamental issues of public policy, a discussion of land reform presents a number of analytical difficulties. Land reform is so intimately related with the whole development process that one feels the need to deal with issues of development in general as well as with those more specifically identified with land reform. And the treatment of these issues on a global basis often requires simplification of very complex and nationally specific experiences. There is no single body of theory which encompasses all the strategic variables.

Land reform is a subject fraught with controversy – intellectually as well as politically. The idea of turning over land and its management to uneducated peasants is seen by some as the road to disaster. Landlords, and many professionals as well, are quick to point out the dire consequences of such a policy – peasants will produce only for their own needs, food prices will soar, economic growth will be arrested, etc. Yet this position is contradicted by historical experience. Confidence in the ability of peasants to rise to the challenge has usually been well placed. But the development of this latent human potential requires an appropriate institutional environment. The creation of such an environment is what land reform is about.

In this book I have tried to suggest the basic theoretical relationships between land reform and economic development. I have drawn from a wide range of studies to provide at least some preliminary testing of these ideas. Research sponsored by the Land Tenure Center over the past nine years provided the basic theoretical framework as well as much of the empirical evidence.

I am particularly indebted to my colleagues Don Kanel and William C. Thiesenhusen for permission to draw extensively from some of their previous writings. I appreciate the very helpful research assistance of Larry Lynch who assembled and summarized data from many of the references cited. Present interpretations are, of course, my own and do not imply agreement by these or other individuals and institutions mentioned below whose assistance and support are gratefully acknowledged.

Philip M. Raup and Don Kanel read an earlier draft of the entire manuscript. Their many helpful comments are deeply appreciated. Others who read drafts of this book or portions of it and whose comments proved very useful are Carlos Castillo, William Thiesenhusen, David Christenson, Nimal Sanderatne, Claudio Barriga and Scott Eddie. I am grateful to John Bielefeldt for his able editorial assistance. Finally, my sincere thanks to Julie Smith for typing the manuscript in final form, and for efficiently managing the innumerable tasks involved in getting a manuscript to press. To the above, and many others of the Land Tenure Center's staff, students and faculty who provided assistance and encouragement, I am most grateful.

I appreciate very much the financial support received from the Land Tenure Center (funded in part by a grant from the US Agency for International Development) and the Department of Agricultural Economics. My thanks also to administrators of the College of Agricultural and Life Sciences and the University of Wisconsin for their interest and helpful cooperation in providing a favourable environment for work on these issues of land reform and economic development.

1 The Role of Land Reform in Development Strategy

Economic development is frequently identified with economic growth – the average annual rate of increase in real output *per capita*. Although increased investments and enlarged markets are basic requirements, development also involves complex processes and procedures of institutional change, redistribution of economic and political power, and concerted, deliberate public policy efforts for redistributing the gains and losses inherent in economic growth. Over time, and largely as a result of economic growth, national objectives must be re-defined. Within the context of the last half of the twentieth century, land reform, employment creation and income distribution have become increasingly pressing issues. If the concept of development is too narrow, important policy questions are often ignored or not even recognized. Thus, development must be broadly conceived as the expansion of opportunities and the enhancement of human capacities needed to exploit them. The reduction of mass poverty, unemployment and inequality are the concomitants of development so conceived (Dorner, 1971b). Seers (1969) has stated the issue well:

The questions to ask about a country's development are therefore: What has been happening to poverty? What has been happening to unemployment? What has been happening to inequality? If all three of these have declined from high levels, then beyond doubt this has been a period of development for the country concerned. If one or two of these central problems have been growing worse, especially if all three have, it would be strange to call the result 'development', even if per capita income doubled (p. 3).

In the early stages of industrialization, agriculture comprises the major activity of a large majority of the population. In most of the less industrialized countries of the world, 50 per cent or more of the population relies directly on agriculture for a livelihood. Thus it is evident that overall development must include – indeed must often begin with – agricultural development. Without the production of a surplus in agriculture (over and above the production required to sustain the workers in agriculture), industrialization cannot occur unless alternative sources of foreign exchange earnings are available from the export of minerals, or from services such as tourism. Agricultural development, like development of the overall economy, includes all the complex processes referred to above – increased investments, improved technology, institutional change, redistribution and redress of the imbalances inherent in these processes, etc. Over time, and as a result of developmental policies, an economic system is transformed from one that is largely agricultural to one in which the industrial sector becomes the dominant one.

Agriculture's role in development

There are a number of contributions that the agricultural sector must make throughout this process of transformation, and there are many interactions and interdependencies between agriculture and industry. Agriculture must provide the food supplies for a growing population and for the increased demand resulting from higher per capita incomes. In many cases agriculture must also produce a surplus for export to finance the capital equipment and other imports needed for development. Lagging production in the agricultural sector can lead to higher food prices, increased imports of food, decreased agricultural exports, or some combination of these effects. Higher food prices in the industrial sector may result in increased wage payments and thereby reduce the savings–investment potential in this sector. Increased food imports or a decrease in agricultural exports would reduce the foreign exchange available for the importation of industrial equipment so essential in the early stages of industrialization.

The agricultural sector must also contribute both capital and labour to the non-agricultural sectors in the process of development. Capital transfers are achieved through a variety of mechanisms: taxation, direct quota deliveries of farm products to the state, rental payments to landlords, farmer savings channelled into industrial investments, migrations, and terms of trade that are unfavourable to farm products *vis-à-vis* manufactured goods. Young people who leave agriculture may represent one of the most important sources of capital transfers. The quantity and quality of capital represented by such migrants depends upon the investments made on their behalf before they leave agriculture. Such capital transfers do not necessarily imply that the income of farmers will fall farther behind that of industrial workers, although this may indeed occur under certain circumstances. If productivity increases more rapidly in the agricultural sector than in the rest of the economy, and if these benefits are widely shared and distributed among the farming population, siphoning some of the surplus from agriculture need not produce a widening rural–urban income gap.

The transfer of manpower from agricultural to non-agricultural occupations is inherent in the overall transformation processes of development. However, the problem of recent decades has been to organize the agricultural sector to hold more labour until such time when this labour can be productively absorbed in other sectors. Finally, agricultural development must provide the increased rural incomes needed to enlarge the demand for industrial products. This serves to stimulate investments in the industrial sector. The complexities of these interactions and their relation to land tenure and reform are explored more fully in later chapters.

Concepts of land tenure and reform

Land tenure institutions and their reform have a direct bearing on questions of development. The land tenure system embodies those legal and contractual or customary arrangements whereby people in farming gain access to productive opportunities on the land. It constitutes the rules and procedures governing the rights, duties, liberties and exposures of individuals and groups in the use and control over the basic resources of land and water. In short, land tenure institutions help to shape the pattern of income distribution in the farm sector (Dorner, 1964; Carroll, 1964). However, land tenure institutions do not exist in isolation. The dimensions and the future security of farming opportunities are critically affected by labour, capital and product markets.

Land reform means changing and restructuring these rules and procedures in an attempt to make the land tenure system consistent with the overall requirements of economic development. In non-industrialized societies, land represents the principal form of wealth and the principal source of economic and political power; the land tenure system reflects social class structures and relations. A restructuring of these rules and procedures involves changes in the political, social and economic power positions of several groups within a society. Changes of such magnitude do not always proceed along rational lines, and the events that follow are frequently uncontrollable and unpredictable. In other words, land reform is not simply a matter on which it is necessary to convince the minister of agriculture or even the political head of the nation. It is not so freely manipulable as the introduction of new crop varieties or changes in the agricultural extension programme, difficult as these may be.

Land reform has an essential core meaning which concerns significant and purposeful changes in land tenure – changes in ownership and control of land and water resources. Specific measures may include: expropriation of large estates and the distribution of land among the tillers, either for individual ownership and operation or for collective use; abolition or improvement in tenancy conditions by converting tenants into owners or by reducing rental payments; issuance of land titles to the tillers to provide them with greater security; and transformation of tribal and other traditional forms of tenure in the interests of the cultivators of the land.

A guiding principle of many land reforms has been that the tillers of the land – the cultivators – must have the opportunity for full participation in determining the procedure by which rights in land are defined, how these rights are exercised, and how they are changed. Conflicts among the several parties holding an interest in a particular tract of land (owner, tenant, labourer, local and state governments) must be subject to impersonal and objective means of adjudication rather than to resolution in a discriminatory manner favouring those individuals or groups with the most influence and power.

Reform and development

Land reform is often viewed as an instrument primarily for the achievement of greater equity and social justice. However, with population often pressing on land resources and with technology opening the way for major advances in the levels of living for all people, reform has the dual purpose of serving as both a redistributive instrument and a vehicle for achieving increased productivity. To achieve the latter, land reform must be accompanied by changes in the pre-reform structure of supporting services – agricultural credit, marketing, research and extension, input supply, and processing and storage. Only through increased productivity *widely shared* can the quality of life of the underprivileged millions be enhanced. Without increases in productivity, redistribution alone will achieve only modest and temporary benefits. Land reform improves the prospects for raising production and productivity since new incentives for increased work and investments are created as a result of the more equitable distribution.

Land tenure reform and its potentialities must be viewed within the overall requirements of development. The redistribution of property rights in land can break down certain rigidities within a society and set the stage for a different organization in the agricultural sector, but it alone will not achieve development (Clark, 1971). Land tenure reform may, however, make it possible for the agricultural sector to contribute in an effective way to overall development objectives. While land reform is not a sufficient measure and needs to be accompanied by many other programmes, it is often essential for providing a stable base for a country's future economic and political development.

Increased urgency of reform

Land reform is becoming increasingly urgent in many of the less-industrialized countries. Many have experienced a deterioration in employment opportunities in both rural and urban sectors. Their rapid population growth has led to increased rural-to-urban migration. Although employment opportunities in the urban sectors are insufficient, the potential benefits indicated by earning differentials as well as by increased access to health and educational services serve as a pull factor in the migration process. Lack of opportunities in the agricultural sector serve as a push factor. The number of stable and permanent employment opportunities in farming is in many cases declining, while seasonal work and the number of migratory workers are increasing (Quiros, 1971; Schmid, 1967). Inequalities in the distribution of income are not narrowing; if anything, income distribution is becoming more skewed (Dandekar and Rath, 1971; Dorner and Felstehausen, 1970). These combined influences have led to increasing social and political tensions and instability in the less-developed countries. Although overall growth rates of agricultural output have been fairly high, especially in certain lines of production, they have been insufficient to provide substantially improved diets for the rapidly growing populations in many of these countries. Furthermore, earnings from agricultural exports in the less-industrialized countries have not increased over the past decade and a half while their imports of agricultural products has almost doubled (Christensen, 1970).

In these factors signalling an increased urgency of reform, the various requirements and dimensions of both reform and of development are evident. Firstly, there are economic requirements of productivity increases, employment creation, a better income distribution, and an agricultural surplus for the generation of capital of both foreign and domestic origin. Secondly, there are social dimensions of improved health, education and other services in the countryside, and breaking up old class structures of the traditional system. Finally, there are the political needs of establishing full economic and political citizenship for the excluded masses and their integration into a cohesive nation which will encourage the creation of a new relationship between them and their government. Land reform and associated institutional changes have an immediate and direct bearing on these requirements. Investment programmes carried out within present land tenure and other institutional structures affect several of these dimensions only tangentially and indirectly or not at all.

Recent development efforts and their lessons

Land reform is not, of course, a modern phenomenon. Peasants have throughout the centuries agitated and fought for more secure rights to the land they tilled.

There is a deep belief among peasants, whose ancestors may have lived for centuries from particular lands, that the lands and waters which have sustained them so long are somehow theirs – in a rightful sense. The remark of an African chief, as reported by . . . Meek, summarizes eloquently the peasants' philosophy of land and civilization: 'I conceive that land belongs to a vast family of which many are dead, few are living, and countless numbers are still unborn' (Meek, 1947). To the individual peasant family their hold on the land has long been both the hallmark of their status and the elementary basis of their survival. With sufficient land of their own, some have lived well; without land countless millions have suffered literal starvation. The peasants' attachment to land is not a mere whim or prejudice; it reflects solid judgements of the requirements for survival which have matured through centuries of precarious and rugged living (Parsons, 1957, p. 214).

Yet land reform as an explicit and strategic developmental issue has gained new prominence in recent decades. The end of the Second World War marks the beginning of a new era. Many states achieved political independence in the two decades following the war's close. Colonialism crumbled and the old powers began a massive dismantling of empire. New national governments came to power with independence from foreign domination and internal development high on the agenda of national priorities. It was the initial phase of what now is commonplace – national plans for active government participation in stimulating economic development.

Politicians, and many economists too, identified industrialization with development and agriculture with backwardness. Development was equated with the industrial world, and to emphasize the development of agriculture was to run the risk of being charged with imperialistic tendencies – a continuing attempt of the industrial powers to retain their dominance over the poor, agrarian countries. The instinct is understandable, and certainly the identification of industry with modernity is appropriate in projecting the final outcome of a long process. But it provides little guidance for current policy. The emphasis on industrialization and the relative neglect of agriculture characterized many of the early development plans. Problems, however, soon became apparent.

The need for more food

Population growth rates in the less-developed countries turned out to be much higher than development planners had anticipated. Rapid population growth accompanied and even preceded development efforts rather than following nineteenth century European patterns where population growth was to a much greater degree a response to development. New technologies in preventive medicine and disease control caused a sharp decline in the death rate in the non-industrialized nations while the birth rate remained at high levels. The assumption of an annual population growth rate of 1 or 1·5 per cent – appropriate for an earlier era – proved wrong. Population in the less-developed countries is now growing at 2 or 3 per cent annually. The demand for food increases accordingly.

A second difficulty resulting from an over-emphasis on industry and a relative neglect of agriculture grew out of the very success of development efforts in the industrial sector. Increases in disposable incomes stimulated the demand for food. Changes in the demand for food are determined largely by population growth, increased *per capita* incomes, and the income elasticity of demand for food (which declines as average incomes rise) (Stevens, 1965).

The income elasticity of demand for food expresses the relationship between the proportionate increase in expenditures for food and the proportionate increase in income. As family incomes rise, a declining proportion of the incremental increase is spent on food. When average incomes are very low, the income elasticity of demand for food may be in the range of 0·6 to 0·8. Therefore, with a 2 per cent increase in per capita incomes, the demand for food will increase at the rate of 1·2 (2×0·6) to 1·6 (2×0·8) in addition to the increase resulting from population growth.[1] With a population growth rate approaching or even exceeding 3 per cent annually, the demand for food in many of the less-industrialized nations is growing at a rate of 4 per cent annually or more.[2] These countries therefore need a considerably larger annual increase in food production than the industrialized countries. The need to earn foreign exchange through farm-produced exports adds to the importance of increasing agricultural production.

The need for more jobs

Increased production, as noted earlier, is only one of the many requirements of agricultural development. Despite the early development emphasis on industrialization, difficulties were experienced in absorbing large increases in the labour force in the relatively small urban sector. Rural population continued to grow, though at a slower rate than total population because of rural-to-urban migration. Much of the very rapidly growing urban population could be absorbed only in precarious, low productivity urban jobs.

Historical evidence shows that the absolute number of rural people declines only in later stages of development (Dovring, 1964). For example, in the United States, the non-farm population exceeded that on farms by the 1880s while the absolute number in farming first reached its peak around 1915. A major and rapid absolute decline in the US farm population did not occur until about 1940. In Japan, this rapid decline in the farm population did not occur until after 1950.

1. The category 'food' is a very general one. The income elasticity of demand varies for individual commodities, and consumer demands change over time as a result of income changes. As *per capita* incomes continue to rise, the demand for some farm products will increase much more rapidly than that for others. Cropping patterns and the output mix in agriculture must change accordingly.

2. This discussion assumes that the rate of growth in *per capita* income is widely shared. If increases in incomes are very unevenly distributed, then the full impact of the income elasticity of demand for food will not be realized. On the other hand, if *per capita* income increases are accompanied by a distribution in favour of low income groups, the food requirements would be further increased. For similar reasons there may not be a one-to-one relationship between growth in numbers of people and increased demand for food.

Given these developmental requirements of increased output and employment, a labour-intensive approach with reliance on yield-increasing technical innovations in the earlier phases of agricultural development seems most appropriate. Such an approach would produce the required increases in agricultural production and avoid displacing labour prematurely It is a prescription for agricultural research (including the development of types of mechanization appropriate to the labour-surplus conditions of most less-developed countries), for large increases in the use of yield-increasing inputs such as fertilizer, improved seeds, insecticides and pesticides, for increases in irrigation facilities, and for building the service institutions in extension, marketing and credit (Johnston and Mellor, 1961).

Mechanization which is basically labour-displacing rather than yield-increasing would be minimized. However, this would not preclude certain types of mechanization which, although labour-displacing to some extent, could also be land-saving, yield-increasing or risk-reducing. Under appropriate private rental, cooperative or state-sponsored arrangements, such mechanization services could be made available to farmers on small farms or to those farming under a cooperative system. Or, as in the case of Japan, special small-scale implements and power sources could be developed for a small-farm agriculture.

At times tillage operations can be more effectively performed with tractor power (deep ploughing) than with human labour and animal power. Improved tillage may have a direct influence on yields. It may be critical to mechanize certain operations in order to encourage and facilitate double cropping. Weather patterns and the crops' growing cycles may restrict the number of days available for preparing land and planting the second crop after harvest of the first crop. Sometimes new high yielding varieties require more timely operations in both planting and harvesting to yield at their increased potential. All these factors must be evaluated, but mechanization that is primarily labour displacing should be restricted.

The green revolution

New technology has been widely recognized as a necessary ingredient in development. In the early years of the new economic development consciousness following the Second World War, it was assumed that technology existing in the industrialized countries could rather easily be transferred to the less-developed countries. It has become increasingly clear, however, that new technology must be developed for or adapted to the climatic, ecological, factor proportion and institutional conditions specific to each country.

Several major breakthroughs in the development of new high yielding varieties, especially of wheat and rice, have been achieved in recent years. These new varieties, along with a package of farming practices including high rates of fertilization and the controlled use of irrigation, have been adopted in selected areas of a number of Asian countries (Falcon, 1970; see also Wharton, 1969, and Brown, 1970). This phenomenon, called the 'green revolution', thus far has had very little impact in Africa or in Latin America outside of Mexico.

The green revolution is, of course, a necessary and sought-for achievement. It offers promise for the more densely populated countries to sustain their growing numbers until they can achieve more effective control of population growth rates and expand their industrial sectors. The threat of impending mass starvation, much discussed especially after the major drought experienced by India in the mid 1960s, has certainly receded.

Despite these positive results, several weaknesses and some of the new problems created by this revolution deserve recognition. The acreage covered by the new varieties is still modest even in countries where they have been planted most extensively. For example, in India where acreage has expanded rapidly, only 7 per cent of the rice acreage and slightly over 25 per cent of the wheat acreage was planted with the new varieties in 1968/69 (Falcon, 1970; see also Barker, 1970, and Dalrymple, 1969). In South and Southeast Asia during the 1968/69 season, about 13 per cent of the rice acreage and 21 per cent of the wheat acreage was covered by the new varieties.

In many cases the controlled use of irrigation required to reap full benefits from these new varieties has led to regional disparities. Even in areas where irrigation is available, owing to the requisite complimentary inputs required, only those farmers having access to credit have been able to adopt and reap the benefits of this new technology. To date, research and experimentation has not been pursued with equal vigour in most other crops or in livestock production. With the uneven development of such new technologies and with the more rapid adoption by the more well-to-do farmers (whose advantage was further enhanced by a favourable price policy), income inequalities have grown. Increased outputs and the eventual downward pressure on prices create additional burdens for the less-favoured farmers, leading to further inequalities and regional disparities. As Ladejinsky (1970) has noted in speaking of India:

Without minimizing the significance of the accomplishments, however, one must say that the revolution is highly 'selective', even if its spread effect is not inconsiderable in certain areas. The green revolution affects the few rather than the many not only because of environmental conditions but because the majority of the farmers lack resources, or are 'institutionally' precluded from taking advantage of the new agricultural trends (pp. 763–4).

It seems reasonable to believe that the green revolution has created employment opportunities, both in agricultural production and in the handling, processing and marketing of the increased output. However, employment opportunities in the production phase may have become more precarious, with less permanent employment (but increased seasonal work) and fewer opportunities for renting land. As land values have risen and the prospects for profit from farming have increased (as a consequence of the increased yield potentials and favourable prices), some landlords have taken their formerly rented lands for operation on their own account with hired labour.

There are too many tenants and sharecroppers to deal with them summarily without courting a good deal of trouble, but the old squeeze whereby tenants are reduced to sharecroppers and eventually to landless workers is being accelerated as more of the bigger owners become involved with the new technology. The basic provisions of tenancy reform are less attainable than before the advent of the green revolution (Ladejinsky, 1970, p. 764).

The new seed varieties and the accompanying technologies are certainly not the primary cause of the accentuated imbalances in the countryside.

It is not the fault of the green revolution that the credit service does not serve those for whom it was originally intended, that the extension service is falling behind expectations, that the village . . . councils are essentially political rather than developmental bodies, that security of tenure is not given to the many, that rentals are exorbitant, that ceilings on land ownership are notional. . . . To a considerable extent these are man-made issues of long standing. Modernization of agriculture should include a combination of technical factors geared to higher production *and* improvements in the institutional framework to benefit the rural underprivileged (Ladejinsky, 1970, p. 766).

Increased productivity alone, when achieved within a tenure structure of great inequalities, does not improve the lives of the great mass of peasants. Frequently a one-sided emphasis on production increases with a neglect of institutional issues has exacerbated existing inequalities. The green revolution, therefore, is no substitute for land reform. *Indeed, reform becomes increasingly imperative as the rate of adoption of new technologies accelerates.*

The rapid introduction of new technology always presents problems of dislocation and tends to undergird the forces leading to inequality in a society. It is indeed a process of 'creative destruction', to use Schumpeter's (1950) famous characterization. These problems are less severe in a relatively open, mobile, opportunity-oriented society than they are in a class structured system with rigid institutions that support these basic inequalities.

New twentieth century conditions

Several new conditions of the late twentieth century were either absent or of a different order of magnitude in the nineteenth and early part of the twentieth centuries. Firstly, science and the technology which it yields are predominantly centred in the industrialized world, and new developments are primarily in response to the problems experienced by the industrialized countries where the factor proportions (especially capital–labour) are quite different from those in the more agrarian, less-industrialized world. In the latter, labour is plentiful and capital (and in many cases also land) is scarce, but new technologies are more nearly geared to the reverse situation. This permits technological leap-frogging – the introduction of production methods and practices from outside (rather than those developed indigenously in response to internal needs and requirements) which very often are capital intensive and labour extensive (Falcon, 1970). The development strategies of the past several decades have in fact encouraged this. Certainly there is a need for capital and machinery imports, but the fact remains that enough appropriate technology is not being developed to fit the factor proportions existing in the developing world.

Secondly, the employment opportunities in industry are more limited today than in the past century because of the capital-intensive nature of contemporary industrial technology. This condition is the more serious because of the rapid population growth rates, especially in areas already very densely populated. Migration to the new world, available to Europe in the nineteenth century, is no longer a major alternative in the less-developed countries of today. Finally, rapid communication has made it possible for people everywhere to view progress – a better life for themselves and their children – as a real possiblity. These new expectations are articulated in new demands that these expectations be fulfilled.

New technology was introduced into traditional societies long before the so-called green revolution. However, the social and institutional structure (dominated by the land tenure system in agrarian societies) did not permit the benefits of this technology to spread widely throughout these societies. Consequently, development was always confined to limited strata of the population. The need for institutional reform arises from the accumulated introduction of technology, and that need existed even before the recent adoption of practices associated with the green revolution. Land tenure and related institutional reforms are often needed to ensure that the rapid introduction of new technology serves as a positive force in economic development – broadly defined.

Obstacles to reform

The economic and political power associated with landed interests is one of the key obstacles to land reform which inevitably involves tough political decisions and confrontations. The complexities and political nature of the process have been well stated by Galbraith (1951):

Unfortunately some of our current discussion of land reform in the underdeveloped countries proceeds as though this reform were something that a government proclaims on any fine morning – that it gives land to the tenants as it might give pensions to old soldiers or as it might reform the administration of justice. In fact a land reform is a revolutionary step; it passes power, property, and status from one group in the community to another. If the government of a country is dominated or strongly influenced by the landholding groups – the one that is losing its prerogatives – no one should expect effective land legislation as an act of grace. . . . The world is composed of many different kinds of people, but those who own land are not so different – whether they live in China, Persia, Mississippi, or Quebec – that they will meet and happily vote themselves out of its possession (pp. 695–6).

Acceptance of the inevitable consequences of a land reform – a redistribution of political power and influence, with the mass of presently excluded farmers gaining a voice in shaping public programmes and policies – clearly implies bold political decisions; and the possibility of getting these decisions often depends on the kind of pressure group activity, especially that of strong peasant organizations, that can be mustered in favour of the reform.

Internal obstacles

In many of the less-developed countries where reforms are needed, there is a lack of rural – tenant, sharecropper, farm labourer, small owner – organizations. This lack of organization often reflects the intolerance of an opposition to such organizations by those who stand to lose if reforms are implemented. Such organizations have often played a major role in carrying out land tenure reforms. Even a government with a strong interest and will to reform the land tenure system will find it difficult to do so without the active participation of local people who know best the circumstances existing in their locality.

In a pre-reform situation it is practically impossible to enforce legislative provisions of rent control and minimum wages without the assistance of strong local organizations. Such organizations can serve to support tenants and labourers and encourage them to report violations of these legislative provisions. This is frequently the only way to get administrative action and results. It is a means of keeping employers and landlords honest. Furthermore, in several Latin American countries land reforms have been carried out in response to peasant land invasions, dramatizing not only the plight but also the potential strength of the peasantry (Brown, 1971a).

A wide variety of obstacles to reform can be grouped under the general heading of ineffective legislation. This category does not include obstructive legislation, such as that prohibiting the organization of rural workers (not an uncommon provision), but laws and administrative procedures established for the explicit purpose of implementing land tenure reforms. Such legislation is sometimes produced under pressure – both internal and external. But so long as those who feel their interests threatened by a genuine reform hold the decisive power, there are many ways of assuring that legislation will be ineffective. Only a few will be mentioned here:

1. Lack of specific criteria for land-taking procedures with resulting delays, litigation and inaction.

2. Requirements that all expropriated land be purchased with immediate cash payment at market prices, with ensuing financial restrictions confining any reform activity to relatively small areas.

3. Primary emphasis on settlement in new areas with the land tenure structure in present productive areas (where most of the infrastructural investments exist) untouched so that present inequalities persist.

4. Preoccupation with consolidating small units rather than reorganizing or redistributing large ones, although such consolidation cannot be achieved without providing more resources for the people in these overcrowded areas. (The same limitation applies also to any attempt at controlling subdivision through inheritance or sale in areas of growing population pressure.)

5. Complex and excessively legalistic procedures.

6. Irregular and inadequate financing provided in national budgets for agencies charged with implementing the reform.

Such legislation often serves to reconfirm the peasants' lack of faith in a government that has always, in their view, acted in bad faith and foreign to their own interests. It may be better to have no land reform law than to have one that further undermines the peasants' confidence in government and that calls into question a government's honesty, sincerity and integrity.

There are other factors which tend to impede implementation of a land reform. Many countries have no records at all or only a very inadequate system concerning land quality, physical location, and land measurement and boundary identification. Such records must be established and verified by the state, and the state must then enforce and protect the registered rights to specific and identifiable property – whether held by an individual or a group. At present, it is often difficult to know or to determine who owns what. This issue is critical in most of the less-developed countries.

Finally, a general lack of relevant statistics presents many problems. Neither national nor international agencies have established systematic statistical series on such critical indicators as employment, income distribution, and regional or local consequences (as opposed to aggregates via national income accounts) of major new investment programmes. In most cases the data could be provided, but their provision has never been judged an item of high priority. Seers (1969) maintains that:

lack of data on poverty, unemployment and inequality reflects the priorities of statistical offices rather than the difficulties of data collection. The conceptual problems of these measures do not seem to be more formidable than those of the national income. We have just grown accustomed to ignoring [them] (p. 3).

External obstacles and failings of international assistance

But internal problems and obstacles, strategic as they are, are not the only ones obstructing effective land reforms. The programmes of international and bilateral assistance agencies also influence the course of development. One of the problems has been the way in which these agencies have conceptualized their task.

Since they have often equated development with increases in output, their capital and technical assistance have gone to those projects promising the highest rate of return. External financing, though ordinarily representing a minor portion of a country's overall development investments, has nevertheless served to draw substantial national resources into projects approved according to these criteria. Calculation of benefit–cost ratios has proceeded on the basis of the existing income distribution, but the impoverished masses have little income and thus their needs are not registered in such calculations. As a result, both internal investments and international capital assistance have tended to concentrate on maximizing production through relatively capital-intensive processes in the modern industrial sector and in the commercial subsector of agriculture. But the restricted distribution of benefits associated with these investment programmes have often led to increased inequalities.

These investment criteria are often grounded in faulty assumptions. They assume that there are close linkages between increases in investments and productivity on the one hand, and employment creation and improved income distribution on the other. Experience has shown that such linkages are not automatic consequences of policies emphasizing economic growth; these linkages must be created through specific policy measures. In the agricultural sector, land reform is one measure for establishing the conditions whereby such linkages can develop. The general strategy followed in the past (without land reform) has proven inadequate, tending to increase inequalities and failing to provide sufficient employment opportunities. In effect, this strategy has all too often favoured those who stand in opposition to land reform.

A final obstacle of external origin is the land and other agricultural enterprises sometimes owned or controlled by foreign interests. This is most frequently found in the sector producing for export. Pressure by these interests and a fear of losing export markets on the part of national governments often serve as a powerful impediment to the reform of the land tenure structure.

Land reforms in historical perspective

This enumeration of problems and obstacles in carrying out land reforms should not suggest that no important land reforms have taken place in recent decades. Several very significant ones occurred in the late 1940s and early 1950s. They were instituted under many different political forms and conditions and with varying degrees of coverage and success: under relatively democratic procedures (India), military regimes (Egypt), military occupations (Japan), peasant revolutions (Bolivia), communist collectivizations (Eastern Europe), and massive revolutionary movements with profound political and economic transformations (mainland China) (Parsons, *et al.*, 1956; Parsons, 1957). These and other reforms of the 1950s and the 1960s in Latin America, Asia, Africa and the Middle East will be cited frequently in later chapters to illustrate problems and accomplishments of reforms.

This final section, however, briefly outlines several historical experiences illustrating the way in which land tenure systems were established and reformed in some of the industrialized countries. These nations found it necessary to restructure their land tenure systems in the process of economic development. At the same time these experiences show that conditions in the past, when these countries transformed their land tenure systems, were very different from those existing in today's less-industrialized nations. These experiences can only be illustrative rather than suggestive of specific policy guides for today's agrarian, less-industrialized nations. Moreover, land tenure institutions are not static. They continue to evolve as they are adapted to changing circumstances in the institutional environment. Land reform implies an abrupt change, yet once new land tenure institutions are established, there is need for flexibility so they can continue to adapt to new circumstances. The following historical sketches will illustrate some of these points.

No tenure system can be judged *best* in the abstract. Any judgement concerning a particular system must take note of the man–land ratio, the existing system of organization in agriculture, the prevailing institutional and technological conditions in the society, the stage at which that society lies in the transformation from an agrarian to an industrial economy, and the goals which specific groups and organizations are attempting to achieve.

The system of European feudalism of several centuries ago appears, under modern conditions, to be without redeeming qualities. Although comprising a total system of political, social and economic institutions, it was at base an agrarian system built around the control of land. Yet despite its inadequacies, its injustices, and its rigidities by modern standards, this feudal system was an adaptation to the times. Growing as it did out of a crumbling and disintegrating world empire, it organized people according to strict and rigid class structures with mutual obligations between classes, thereby assuring some degree of internal harmony and a measure of security from potential enemies external to the feudal manor (Dorner and Kanel, 1971).

But the feudal system came into conflict with the evolving goal of creating strong nation states; proved ill-equipped to respond to the requirements of expanding markets; was too inflexible to accommodate the increased use of capital; and failed to meet the needs of man's evolving conception of himself. It was inconsistent with the requirements of making the great change from an agrarian system to an industrial society. Reforming these agrarian systems from the seventeenth through the nineteenth centuries was part of the general social revolution that accompanied industrialization in western and central Europe.

Despite many reform efforts throughout the nineteenth century, the Russian land tenure system retained many of its feudal characteristics up to the twentieth century. This system was thoroughly transformed in the 1920s and 1930s. Russian collectivization may not have provided the individual incentives or the decision-making freedom of a family-farm system, but the major concern of Soviet planners was rapid industrialization. Russian agriculture was producing a substantial export surplus at the time of collectivization. A major requirement was to free labour from work in agriculture in order to provide the manpower for the new factories. In addition, the state had to 'squeeze' some of the surplus production from the agricultural sector to secure a relatively cheap supply of food for the growing population in the industrial sector. Of course, collectivization of agriculture was perhaps necessary to assure party control over the economic system and to prevent decentralized political developments. The collective system functioned to achieve these ends (Owen, 1966; Nicholls, 1964; Nove, 1971). In recent years new production incentives have been introduced, presumably because the system was not achieving present objectives and goals.

When the design of a US system of land tenure and economic organization of agriculture was being debated, the major alternative to family farms appeared to be a system of large estates and plantations with some features of European feudalism. The latter had been and was being challenged on both political and economic grounds and was in various stages of disintegration. Furthermore, the large land mass to the west had to be secured from threats by other nations. The family-farm system was perhaps the only reasonable alternative by which a relatively weak government, lacking major communication and transportation networks, could assure that this large land mass would be rapidly settled and incorporated into the nation.

US development also required production of an agricultural surplus and the release of labour from agriculture to meet the demands of the growing industrial sector. But the means employed were entirely different from those used by the Soviet Union a century later. The United States placed primary emphasis on new technology to increase the productivity of land and especially the productivity of labour, and relied on immigration and the competition among many small producers for allocation of production factors among alternative uses (Owen, 1966).

Throughout the nineteenth century the United States was characterized by a low man–land ratio; except during the period of massive immigration, which was encouraged, population growth was low relative to the experience of most of today's less-developed countries. Furthermore, industrialization in the nineteenth century and the first half of the twentieth was more labour absorptive than it is today. When the Soviet system was instituted about forty years ago, Russia also had a low man–land ratio and a relatively slow population growth. The circumstances surrounding both US and Soviet development are in sharp contrast with current situations in South and Southeast Asia, Latin America and Africa. Rapid population growth rates of recent decades (and capital-intensive, low labour-absorptive industrialization) make it imperative that the agricultural sector hold people rather than being forced to release them.

Thus the nature of the land reform issue facing the less-developed countries today is different from that confronted by Europe in the seventeenth to nineteenth centuries, by the US in the eighteenth and nineteenth centuries,[3] and by Soviet Russia in this century. Land tenure systems reflect specific historical, geographic, economic, social and political conditions. They are continually modified in the process of economic development. For example, in the short period of the past thirty years, US agriculture has been substantially reorganized. The number of farms is less than half of what it was thirty years ago. The eighty-acre and even the 160-acre farm is an inefficient unit for most types of farming in the United States today. While farms in this size range were viable going concerns until about thirty years ago, present technology and factor costs and availabilities make such units inefficient in terms of labour productivity. And since labour is relatively scarce compared with land and capital, labour productivity is

3. The Civil War in the 1860s was also essentially an issue of land reform (see Conrad and Meyer, 1964, and Moore, 1966).

a reasonably good measure for judging efficiency under US conditions (Dorner and Kanel, 1971).[4]

These short descriptions relating tenure systems to concurrent conditions are not intended to imply a neat, logical or simple relationship. Changes in tenure systems emerge out of conflict among contending groups – witness the Soviet debates over the rapidity and method of industrialization and the many US experiments with land settlement policies in the nineteenth century. Tenure systems, as hammered out by experience and conflict, are adaptations to prevailing circumstances and the dominant ideas and political philosophy. Great caution, and at times restraint, are needed so as not to prescribe transplantation of such systems to other areas on the basis of their achievements elsewhere, in an earlier time, or under conditions which no longer exist or cannot be duplicated. Likewise, the specific reference to individual ownership on the one hand and collective farming on the other are oversimplifications of the options available in tenure reforms. There is no reason to believe that countries need to end up with *either* one system *or* another. There is room for and indeed need for diversity and flexibility to accommodate changing circumstances.

Specific tenure arrangements throughout the less-developed world vary widely, and it is difficult to treat the issues of land reform in a general way, especially in trying to connect these issues with those of economic development. The next chapter, however, will elaborate on these differences and point out some specific issues that arise in implementing land reforms, using case studies from a number of countries to illustrate the variations in agricultural situations and in land tenure reforms.

4. Of course, labour productivity as a measure of efficiency in the agricultural sector ignores the social costs of people becoming stranded in rural communities and of large numbers of unskilled workers migrating to cities but failing to find employment within the occupational structure, which is largely determined by the technological developments in industry. These are serious problems in the United States, and they are likely to become all but insoluble in the less-developed countries if means cannot be found to hold more people in agricultural employment (Thiesenhusen, 1969; also President's National Advisory Commission on Rural Poverty, 1967).

2 Diversity in Tenure Issues and Approaches to Reform

One of the most impressive features of the less-industrialized nations is the variety of agricultural conditions and institutional arrangements. Unlike the large cities throughout the world where modern technology – especially in transportation, communications, basic industries and manufacturing – has produced a measure of uniformity, a wide spectrum of conditions prevails in the rural sectors. These variations have many dimensions, and each of these has special bearings on the problems and prospects of land tenure reforms and their impact on development.

The three regions of Africa, Asia and Latin America provide many examples of the diversity in existing agrarian structures. Africa in this context refers to sub-Sahara Africa. Most of the countries in this region have only in recent years won their independence from the colonial powers. The integration of diverse population groups into a cohesive nation and self-government as nation states are relatively new experiences. Many of these new governments, in trying to implement development plans, find their claims to sovereign authority challenged by local, traditional tribal authorities. Until recently most positions of skill and responsibility were occupied by non-Africans, and trained and skilled manpower is still in short supply. A number of Asian countries, too, emerged from colonial rule only in recent decades. However, most Latin American nations have been independent for well over a century. Culturally, the experience within certain areas of all three regions ranges from primitive, orally transmitted traditions to highly developed civilizations with literature and complex legal and social institutions rooted in an ancient past.

The colonial experiences of these regions were also quite different. These differences are still evident today and constitute important elements for framing national development policies. In Africa, European-drawn demarcations sometimes cut across ethnic boundaries. This has at times been a source of hostility and conflict between neighbours and certain ethnic groupings (Christodoulou, 1966). European concepts of land tenure and ownership were introduced in areas of plantation crops, but also in some areas of general farming where private land concessions were granted. On the other hand, in the hinterland areas the traditional, customary practices of dealing with land were undisturbed and remain so down to the present.

In much of Asia colonialism had a profound impact on agrarian structures and village organization. The Europeans frequently introduced a high degree of administrative centralization (often for political reasons). In some cases the traditional local authorities of the village communities had little role to play and consequently their authority often languished. Sometimes colonial administrators installed special tax collectors who later came to be recognized as the proprietors of the land. In other cases large estates were assigned to members of the local aristocracy as rewards for their cooperation. These actions 'resulted in the Zamindari system in India and Pakistan, the haciendas in the Philippines, and the big landed estates in Vietnam' (FAO Regional Office, 1970, p. 5).

In much of Latin America, the present tenure structures originated with the Spanish colonial system, and these basic forms were reinforced after independence from the Spanish Crown. Large land grants to the early colonizers set the pattern for a system dominated by the *latifundia* (including large plantations, traditional *haciendas*, and large cattle *estancias*) and by *minifundia* (extremely small holdings) whose occupants provided much of the labour for the large estates. The consequences of colonial policy were, however, quite different in areas with a large pre-conquest indigenous population in contrast to those areas with a relatively scattered and sparse native population.

These sketches show some of the historical factors underlying the variability of conditions in the less-industrialized countries. Only at the most abstract level can one speak of general development policies under such diverse conditions.

The formulation of development strategies becomes even more complex and requires yet more understanding of local conditions when a major issue is land reform – an area of policy dealing with the intricate and varied institutions of land tenure.

The diversity of existing land tenure institutions

Present tenure and land holding patterns present a baffling array of arrangements. Many countries have small islands of high productivity using modern technology, frequently (although not exclusively) in areas of plantation crops grown for export. In some countries a significant proportion of such plantations are foreign owned or controlled. These plantations have in some cases been nationalized and are now operated as state corporations. Sometimes the fear of losing access to foreign markets has restrained national governments from taking such action.

In traditional, customary tenure systems, the basic or sovereign ownership of land is vested in the local group or tribe. Individuals have only usufructory rights, and these rights can be claimed by persons by reason of their membership in the group (Parsons, 1971). Since one is entitled to inherit a share of family land as a birthright, one does not lose this right by living away from the home village. Although strangers (non-members) may receive land allotments, they do not have the same privileges, especially regarding inheritance of land by their children.

A basic rule of customary tenure is that rights in land are not alienable; ordinarily land cannot be sold or mortgaged (Parsons, 1971). Land is seldom looked upon as a commodity; it is not regarded as being for purchase or sale; land is regarded as community property and exploited in kinship units.

In a country [Nigeria] dominated by tribal groupings the social group, especially the family, is the perpetuating unit – not the land itself. . . . land may be used by a private individual and his immediate family, but not without the consent of his social group. . . . Within this social relationship, the 'owner' of the land has all the privileges we refer to as rights in *fee simple*, except that of sale (Johnson, 1963, p. 8).

In Asia one also finds areas of tribal lands and customary tenures, but this is not the dominating and prevailing feature. Far-reaching legislative enactments of colonial administrations and the relatively long periods of colonial rule transformed the conceptions underlying the traditional agrarian systems, and individualized property in land is widespread. Landlords own much of the land, which is farmed by sharecroppers and tenants in small, independently operated units (except where major land reforms have been carried out). This has sometimes been referred to as the 'rent collection system' of Asian peasant agriculture (Long, 1962). This tenure pattern explains the relative ease by which land reforms achieved a transition to owner-operated family farming in such countries as Japan and Taiwan.

In Latin America there are also some traditional forms of land tenure in the Indian communities of the Andean countries. The Mexican *ejido*, a communal type of tenure created by that nation's land reform, was intended to reconstruct and build upon a traditional form. In the *ejidos* land is communally held and inalienable, but most of it is worked by individual families in small units. In all Latin American countries there are areas where family-sized farms exist; in some local areas they are the predominant form of agricultural exploitation. Nevertheless – again with important exceptions where basic reforms have been carried out as in Mexico, Bolivia and Cuba[1] – the dominating features continue to be the large estates (holding most of the agricultural land resources), and the small, sub-family units (holding relatively little land but serving as a refuge for most of the rural population). Many of the large estates are still managed and farmed as units with hired labour and/or some variant of the traditional system rather than under a sharecropping or tenancy system. Under the traditional system, farm workers have their homes on the estate and receive certain land use privileges in return for work on the estate.

In addition to these general differences which characterize the several world regions, a number of more specific conditions

1. A substantial restructuring of the land tenure system has also occurred in Venezuela, and major reforms are in process in Chile and Peru.

also affect the prospects of land reform. One of these is the man–land ratio, a measure of the population pressure on the land resource.[2] This pressure is greatest in Asia and least in Africa, with Latin America in an intermediate position. For practical purposes, however, this generally has little meaning since mass migrations between these world regions are unlikely to occur. However, nation states are not closed systems, and capital and product flows in international trade can help to equalize opportunities even if there are restrictions on labour flows. The population density does of course affect the developmental options open to individual nations.

Of greater interest and significance are the differences in man–land relationships within regions and especially within individual countries. Here there may be greater scope for the movement of people into less densely populated areas. This is certainly occurring in some areas of Bolivia and Peru where people are migrating from the densely populated highland areas to the lowlands on the eastern side of the Andean mountains. Migrations also occurred from densely populated El Salvador into the less densely populated Honduras. These migrations were generated largely as a result of the expansion of cotton acreage in El Salvador which displaced many peasants from their farms. But this resettlement led to many frictions and eventually to armed conflict after which most of the migrants were again forced back to El Salvador.

While Java in Indonesia, Luzon in the Philippines, and the rice lands of the wet zone in the southwest of Ceylon are among the most densely populated areas of Asia, some of the outer islands of Indonesia, the southern island of Mindanao in the Philippines, as well as the north-central and eastern areas of the dry zone in Ceylon are characterized by relatively low population densities. Here cultivation could be, and in some cases is being, extended. However, this is usually achieved at very high costs since these areas are often lacking in basic infrastructure and are far removed from the nation's

2. This ratio is not very revealing if total land is used as a base. The productive potential of the land, its accessibility, the magnitude of investments and the relative risks involved in its development need to be evaluated.

major markets. Within the African nations, some tribal groups are crowded within their historically defined boundaries, while others may have a great abundance of land. Pressure on the land is growing in most countries because of the rapid growth of population, especially over the past several decades, and because the absolute numbers dependent on agriculture continue to increase.

The degree of land ownership concentration also varies widely. In Latin American countries about 3–4 per cent of the landowners with the largest holdings own 60–80 per cent of the agricultural land (Sternberg, 1971). This pattern is common to most countries in the region except where major land reforms have been carried out. Some Asian countries likewise show substantial degrees of ownership concentration, but operatorship is usually decentralized through sharecropping and tenancy.

In Asia, the size of land holdings is of a different order of magnitude than in Latin America. Wheras the large units in Latin America may have 500 to 1000 or more hectares of arable land, those in Asia are more likely to fall within the 50 to 100 hectare range. For example, in Ceylon (1962), land ownership units above 50 acres (about 20 hectares) represented 33 per cent of the total land area. In India (1960–61), ownerships above 25 acres represented only 31 per cent of all land. Figures for Pakistan are fairly similar to those for India (Ahmad and Sternberg, 1971).[3] Comparable figures for sub-Sahara Africa are not available, and they would have little meaning within the present customary system.

An additional point of contrast lies in climatic conditions and the type of agriculture to which they give rise. Slash and burn agriculture or shifting cultivation is common in most tropical regions. A piece of land is cleared of trees and brush. The ash remaining from burning this debris serves to fertilize the soil. After several years of cropping, the land is 'allowed to rest' for a number of years during which it again grows up in trees and brush. Usually the length of the fallow period varies inversely with the population density. In many parts of

3. Actual concentration may be greater than these figures indicate since census enumerations tend to understate ownership concentration.

Africa, this system, along with inheritance, multiple wives, and deliberate attempts to have land of different types as insurance against drought or flood, has led to much splintering and fragmentation of land holdings. In some of the more arid regions, by contrast, nomadic tribes roam over large areas with their animal herds – a pattern of life especially prevalent in parts of the Middle East and North Africa.

In much of Asia and Latin America, private property interests are strong and individualized property in land is the rule. Great economic, social and cultural cleavages exist between a prosperous land-owning elite and the mass of peasants with little or no land. These features are not entirely absent from the African scene. However, in much of Africa the key problem is to transform a traditional, customary land tenure system. This system has performed reasonably well as a mechanism of group survival under economic conditions not much above subsistence levels. But new arrangements must be worked out, if possible building upon elements within the present system, that are consistent with the capitalization and technological requirements of increased productivity. This is not to say that Africans can ignore the land tenure questions common to other regions. Indeed, there are already some instances of land concentration in the hands of the strong and the aggressive who were in a position to take advantage of the combined forces of increased population and the introduction of new technology. There is always a possibility that a *latifundia* type of feudalism could evolve as happened with some of the tribal institutions in parts of the Middle East.[4]

Two major issues in reform:
land acquisition and tenure reorganization

The previous sections highlighted some of the existing differences among the less-industrialized countries and regions of the world. It is evident that no single policy formula will be appropriate under these widely varying conditions. Nor can

4. For a more elaborate analysis of these complex differences by world regions, see the United Nations reports on progress in land reform (United Nations, 1970). I have also included only scattered references to the Near and Middle East, an area which presents still another set of unique circumstances. For a review of this region, see El Ghonemy (1968).

such policy be simply prescribed on the basis of ideological dicta. The formulation of land reform and development policies must be based on knowledge of a country's resources, its people, and its institutions. As a consequence of some of these inherent differences, the approaches to land reform have also varied widely. These variations can be illustrated by the way in which different nations have dealt with two major issues which must be addressed in any land reform effort. The first issue concerns the ways in which the state has and can acquire land, while the second one deals with the alternative post-reform land tenure systems established.

Land acquisition

The method by which land has been acquired for redistribution has taken many forms in different countries. Confiscation of lands by the state without compensation to former owners has been one means of land acquisition. The land reforms in most of the communist countries were of this nature. Uncompensated acquisition, however, has also been the policy with respect to at least certain lands in most countries carrying out basic reforms.

The initial distribution of land in Egypt following the 1952 reform law included over 450,000 acres confiscated from the royal family (Food and Agricultural Organization report, 1971). Land holdings of foreigners are frequently the object of confiscation, especially in cases where national independence is preceded by armed conflict (e.g. land held by the French in Algeria). Sometimes a key sector, or crop, is dominated by foreign control and becomes the object of confiscation following a radical change in government (e.g. the sugar cane lands and associated facilities owned by United States companies in Cuba). Sometimes compensation is provided by law, but ensuing inflation erodes the value of the delayed payments (bonds or other instruments issued by the state). In the land reform of Japan following the Second World War, payment to landlords greatly depreciated in real terms due to the rampant inflation (Voelkner, 1970, p. 51). The principle of full compensation to former landowners was also not followed in Mexico's land reform.

Foreign landowners (mainly North American) were dispossessed of all their landholdings in Mexico . . . and they were paid, apparently, somewhat less than half of the estimated value of the land. Mexican landowners were on the whole treated even less kindly . . . and only a small minority were ever paid anything, and these at a fraction of the market value of the land that was taken from them (Dovring, 1970, pp. 23–4).

Another major method of land acquisition is expropriation of privately held lands with compensation by the state. The reforms of Japan and Mexico could be included here; they were cited above to illustrate that intended compensation does not always materialize and in effect such expropriation becomes at least partial confiscation (Karst, 1964). Some countries have legislative provisions offering protection against inflation for bonds issued to acquire land. The land reform legislation in Chile, for example, has such a provision. In Taiwan, the value of bonds received by former landowners was expressed in terms of physical commodities. Thirty per cent of the compensation was in the form of stocks in several government-owned industrial enterprises.

Expropriation can be and usually is an extremely complex process. One requisite is the establishment of clearly definable criteria for expropriation. Exemptions based on superior management or productivity ordinarily lead to confusion, delays, long drawn out court cases and little reform. A maximum size limit on the amount of land one family or individual can hold is a common feature of land reform laws.

In the early phases of the land reforms in Eastern Europe following the Second World War, a maximum limit was placed on the amount of land a family could own. Generally this limit was defined in terms of a unit which could be operated by the farmer with his own and his family's labour, i.e. the general conception of a family farm. In Egypt, the limits were first established in 1952 at 200 acres per holding but were reduced to 100 acres in 1961 and to 50 acres in 1969.

The land reform in Egypt was applied to areas (covering about one sixth of the total agricultural land) dependent on irrigation and therefore reasonably uniform in terms of land quality. However, maximum ceiling limits must be varied if land differs widely in quality and productivity. For example, in Chile all land in holdings exceeding '80 basic irrigated hectares' (as defined by law) is subject to expropriation. Given the wide variation in land quality, type of farming, and access to irrigation, the ceiling varies from thirty hectares in the most fertile, irrigated areas to 10,000 hectares in some of the arid and mountainous regions. In India, land policy comes under the jurisdiction of the individual states. Most of them have ceiling legislation limiting the amount of land an individual can own. Here, as elsewhere, immediate family members and other relatives tend to 'subdivide' on paper and thus evade the intent of the legal provisions. Various groups in India now advocate legislative revision to place limits on the holdings of a family rather than on those of an individual.

Where property ownership is highly concentrated, as in much of Latin America, an effective and substantial reform requires that the bulk of privately owned rural property be subject to expropriation. If the reform is too sporadic, piecemeal and scattered over space and time, it creates too much uncertainty for agricultural investments and gives the entrenched powers time to muster their forces to defeat the reform. Not only should most land be subject to expropriation, but there must be a 'quick-taking procedure which enables the reform agency to obtain possession of the land in the shortest time possible, while at the same time providing affected landowners with adequate legal remedies' (Thome, 1971a). Furthermore, as discussed later, marketing, credit and other farm services need to be reorganized to serve the reformed tenure system. This reorganization is not likely to be accomplished unless the land reform is widespread and carried out in a relatively short period of time.

Reforms must establish a compensation scheme of deferred payments based on valuations other than market prices existing before the reform (Thome, 1971a). If compensation is at full market value, it may be impossible to meet the distributional requirements of reform. Thus, in this sense land reform must always be in part confiscatory. However, whether payments for land are indeed 'unreasonable' is a matter to be judged in terms of historical circumstances. Present owners or their ancestors often gained access and ownership to the land by reason of their favoured power position. In many cases present market value reflects investments in infrastructure, much of it created either by the underpaid labourers who are the reform's intended beneficiaries, or through government investments financed by general tax revenues only part of which were collected from present landowners.

The size of any reserve which the former owners of large estates are permitted to retain is of critical importance. If reserves are large relative to the expropriated portion, then these owners will continue to wield important influence and will in effect continue to out-compete the reformed and small-farm sector for the limited resources of credit, technical assistance, marketing and storage facilities, etc. Large estate owners in Mexico were permitted to retain a rather generous reserve for their own use, and they were indeed the major beneficiaries of subsequent government irrigation investments and of credit resources allocated to the agricultural sector. In Bolivia the peasants took control of the lands and many landlords fled to the towns, but the law permitted a substantial reserve for those farms not classified as *latifundia*. This has in subsequent years led to serious conflicts between former owners and peasants – some landlords tried to repossess the land they lost; others sold fictitious titles to peasants. The reserve must be kept relatively small so that man–land relationships on the retained reserve and those on the reformed lands do not differ too greatly.

Confiscation and expropriation, then, have been the major means of land acquisition for land reform purposes. In some cases, for example in Chile, the government used lands acquired in the past and transformed them from government run estates into individual family farms (Thiesenhusen, 1966b). In yet other cases major reliance has been on cash purchase of land for redistribution. Governments, however, do not have the means to accomplish much in this way except for those few cases in which revenues obtained from oil or other mineral exports were sufficiently large, e.g. Venezuela and Iran. Some non-government reform efforts, such as the one by the Catholic Church in Chile, have distributed land to farm workers

(Thiesenhusen, 1966b). At times, owners of large estates, sometimes because of the fear of expropriation, have subdivided and
sold their land in parcels of family-farm or larger sizes (Brown,
1971b). Settlement on public lands has often been encouraged,
sometimes under heavy government subsidy and supervision,
and at other times with a minimum of government help
(Domike, 1970; Thiesenhusen, 1971b). But all these efforts
have been at best supplementary to a more fundamental reform. These efforts alone leave the basic land tenure structures
in the settled – frequently the most productive – agricultural
regions relatively unchanged. Without changes in these latter
regions, the intended redistributional consequences cannot be
achieved.

Post-reform organization of agriculture

The second salient issue in land reform is what kind of organization to establish in the reformed agriculture. Three general
categories or tenure forms will be illustrated by the experiences
of a number of countries: family-farm units retaining private
operating initiative; group farming; and state farms.

1. Private family farms. Frequently family-farm units with
private operating initiative have been retained or created in the
process of reform. Tenancy regulation and rent reduction and
control have been elements in some land reform legislation.
These have ordinarily been most effective when combined with
other measures of a more radical nature, when a strong political will at the highest level of government had a firm conviction
to carry reforms to completion, where adequate governmental
administrative resources were available to implement legal
provisions, and where strong peasant organizations existed or
were created to protect the interests of the tenants against the
greater power of the landlords. These combined positive forces
are not always present.

A case in point, however, is Taiwan. There the land reform
of the late 1940s and early 1950s was carried out in three stages:
first, rent reduction; second, sale of publicly owned lands; and
finally a land-to-the-tiller programme under which landlords
were forced to sell land in excess of certain maximum holdings.

Local farmer organizations played an important role in the implementation of the reform in its several stages.

In commenting on the reforms in Japan and Taiwan, Millikan and Hapgood (1967) point out that

There are never enough bureaucrats and reform experts to go around; the experts become experts in the process of applying the reform. If a reform is to be carried out successfully, it must win the active participation of the people directly affected by the reform, the farmers, who best know the conditions of their rural community; the principle of local involvement applies to land reform just as it does to the other aspects of agricultural development. This has not been recognized by most countries currently engaged in reform activities. . . . So long as the would-be beneficiaries are treated as mere onlookers – the case in most reforms – the reform has little hope of success. The paternalistic assumption that only white-collar officials can administer a reform reflects elitist attitudes that are a handicap to agricultural growth in general (pp. 104–6).

Active involvement and participation of farmers can of course take many different forms, and it does not depend on a system of private property in family-farm units for its expression. In some cases peasant organizations have been less active and involved in the reform process than in Taiwan and Japan. Such was the case in Egypt, but here the other two elements, indispensable for an orderly and effective reform were present – a strong political will at the top and well organized governmental administrative structures to carry out the legal provisions of the law. An additional factor of critical importance for the efficient implementation of the land reforms in Egypt, Japan and Taiwan was the existence of an up-to-date system of land records and property titles.

The land reform in Egypt presents an interesting variation of family-farm operating units with some functions and decisions collectivized or performed by government technicians. The beneficiaries of the reform were required to join local cooperatives. These land reform cooperatives perform a number of the usual functions such as purchasing and distributing production inputs as well as serving as a collecting point through which all farm produce is marketed. Government technicians have played a major role in administering and managing these cooperatives, although more of the functions are now being turned over to the farmers themselves, making the cooperatives more autonomous and independent of government.

An interesting feature is the system of block land use which these cooperatives have developed. The entire area served by one cooperative is divided into three blocks of approximately equal size and managed under a three-year rotation system. The individual land holder, whether tenant or owner, must comply with this rotation scheme. In any particular year all the land in a block is planted to the same crop or crop sequence. This provision is especially important for efficiency in the use of irrigation water, and for the mechanization of certain tillage and crop spraying operations. Since each farmer needs food crops every year, whereas in any given year his entire holding might be planted to cotton or clover, individual farmers exchange use of lands among the blocks in order to obtain the needed products not grown on their own land in that particular year (Platt, 1970; Marei, 1969). 'The block system thus circumvents the physical problems of using fragmented ownerships by combining them into tracts of efficient management size' (Platt, 1970, p. 47). Under this system farmers retain private ownership of their farms and the produce they grow, but certain functions and decisions have been socialized.

Another interesting case of shared management with the retention of family units and private initiative is the Gezira scheme in the Sudan. Here, in the early stages of the scheme's development, the government announced that it would take over all the land required for irrigation in the Gezira and pay rental fees to the former identifiable owners (ownership claims ranged from a fraction of an acre up to 3000 acres.) The land was then divided into family-farm units, and all farmers within the scheme became tenants of the project. A fixed rotation assigns about one-third of the land to cotton each year. The production, harvesting and marketing of the cotton crop is regulated by practices prescribed by the technicians serving under the governing board of the Gezira. On the remainder of the land, the scheme's tenants are free to grow food and fodder crops which they may manage and dispose of at will. The revenue from cotton production is presently divided as follows (this division has undergone considerable change and modification over the years): 36 per cent for the government as payment for the use of land and water; 50 per cent for the tenant for his labour and the inputs he supplies; 2 per cent for local governments as compensation for the tax exemption enjoyed by the leaseholders; 2 per cent for a Social Development Fund; and 10 per cent for the Gezira Board as payment for its administrative and technical services (Gaitskell, 1971).

The above illustrations demonstrate that at times land reforms can retain or create private operating initiative and family farms in more or less their standard and conventional form (Japan and Taiwan), or it can modify the form to include certain decisions under some kind of collective or project management (Egypt and the Gezira scheme in the Sudan). The latter can be considered intermediate forms between private property and family farms on the one hand, and 'group farming' on the other.

One other land reform experience which should be included with the cases where family-farm units are established is that of settlement in new areas or resettlement of people in previously established farming areas. Among the latter is the Million Acre Scheme in Kenya. From 1961 to 1968, over one million acres of land were purchased by the government and parcelled out to over 30,000 African families.

Large European settlements (mainly British) and the establishment of private property in land have been more characteristic here than in most of the other African countries. The colonial government initiated, and the independent government of Kenya has continued, a broad-based programme of land reform in African areas – consolidating and enclosing African lands, and changing the land tenure structure to provide individualized legal title to newly enclosed and consolidated plots (Herz, 1970, p. 6).

The Million Acre Scheme, however, was directed at settling Africans on European-held lands. Although because of the way the land redistribution was carried out (high density and low density schemes with some fairly large land allocations to individual families) the inequalities among the newly settled

African farmers with respect to size of land holding and income are quite severe.

Land settlement in new areas is a part of the land policy of most countries having an agricultural frontier. Sometimes government assistance is limited to construction of roads and a minimum of other infrastructural works, and self-selection of new settlers and spontaneous movement is relied upon. At other times very large investments are incurred in the clearing of land, building of settler houses, etc., with settlers selected by a variety of criteria – usually age, family size, experience in farming, and whether or not they own any land. A problem in many directed settlements has been the high cost of such schemes and the relatively small number of people benefited. In many of the Latin American colonization programmes, cost per farm unit established has averaged $5000 to $6000 or more.

Several distinctions must be made in evaluating land settlement or colonization programs. Brazil, Colombia, the Central American countries and others have emphasized settlement in new areas with a minimum of restructuring in the land tenure patterns existing in the settled areas. These latter areas contain the best lands and most of the infrastructural investments. Colonization or settlement has been used in an attempt to relieve some of the population pressure in the old settled areas while leaving the basic land tenure structures in these areas untouched. However, many times the large farm pattern again emerges in the newly settled regions (Thiesenhusen, 1971b; Domike, 1970).

In contrast is the programme of relocation and controlled resettlement in Ceylon, a country with very limited possibilities for creating new opportunities in its densely settled rice growing areas of the southwest (although effective rent controls, greater tenure security, and conversion of sharecropping to leasing and/or ownership could greatly improve the situation for some of the most disadvantaged cultivators). But in the eastern and north-central provinces of the island, the population density is much lower. Here major new irrigation and reclamation projects have been completed, more are under way, and a substantial number of people have been and more will be resettled in these areas on small family farms with secure title to the land.

2. Group farming – cooperatives and collectives. Apart from land reforms which have retained or created, sometimes in modified form, a family-farm system with private operator initiative are the reforms which have established another form of economic organization in agriculture – group farming with some form of cooperative-collective management. The wide range of conditions under which group farming has been established and the intricate nature of the arrangements makes generalization impossible. Again we shall simply refer to a few experiences for illustrative purposes.

In most of the countries of Eastern Europe[5] following the Second World War, land reform was implemented in several stages. A maximum limit was placed on the area that an individual family could retain as private property, and the land thus acquired by the state was distributed in small farm units; sharecropping was generally eliminated and prohibited; and the training of a large number of agricultural technicians to work in the countryside was emphasized. This was later followed by a movement toward the socialization of agriculture, with the establishment of state farms and collectives accompanied by a concerted effort of industrialization. Although voluntary in principle, joining the collective-cooperative farming structure was influenced by a strong educational-propaganda campaign undertaken by the government and supported by various policy incentives. The latter, of course, sometimes included certain measures of compulsion, such as the graduated 'penalty' delivery quotas imposed on the larger peasant farms.

Rumania provides an example of the transformation to group farming (the state farms will be discussed later). The process of cooperativization or collectivization passed through several stages. First, for some specifically designated crops, e.g. potatoes and sugar beets, jointly utilized machinery was

5. In speaking of Eastern Europe, Poland and Yugoslavia should be considered separately since in these countries individually operated family farms predominate, although they are supported by an elaborate cooperative service structure.

introduced. Ploughing, sowing and harvesting were performed through the cooperative utilization of machinery, but each farmer has his own individual produce to dispose of as he wished. A second and more complex form extended this use of machinery to other crops, and included more collective management and controls. In a third stage, peasants pooled their land for joint operation and all produce was handled and marketed collectively. Peasants received payment for their labour contribution, but they also received a bonus in proportion to the amount of land contributed to the cooperative. In the final stage, payment was based solely on an individual's labour contribution. Land had become common property without additional bonuses paid to former owners and without compensation for the land so contributed.

Theoretically, individuals could choose not to join the cooperative and were given the choice of access to an equivalent amount of land elsewhere. There are even today a scattering of individually operated farms around the collectivized areas. However, most individual farmers joined since to refuse meant to suffer from the discriminatory manner in which all government services were provided. Farm policies – credit, marketing, technical assistance, input supply – all created incentives to join and distinct disadvantages not to join.

In recent years Rumania has moved toward an even more complex form of collectivization – inter-cooperative coordination, investments and the creation of joint enterprises. In early 1971 over 350 of these joint inter-cooperative organizations were in existence. Some of these are very large and highly capital intensive, specializing in hogs, poultry and greenhouse production – often with the necessary processing agri-industrial enterprises combined with the production enterprises.

Two instances of group farming experiments in Africa, which were established in the 1960s, are those in Tanzania and Dahomey. Both are new and evolving programmes which may change substantially in the future. But the initial forms are nevertheless interesting and illustrative of additional types of group farming in an environment quite different from that in Eastern Europe.

The land tenure policy of Tanzania has shifted away from the earlier programmes of establishing freeholds (under German and later British administration) to a policy of long-term leaseholds within a nationalized ownership of land (Parsons, 1971, pp. 75–6). However, at present this emphasis applies only to about one tenth of the country's agricultural land while the remaining lands continue subject to the customary forms of tenure.

The basic policy declared for the country is one of villagization – the policy of *Ujamaa* which retains the traditional concept of communal cooperation and sharing. The *Ujamaa* village is expected to retain the good of the old tribal system but incorporate the good of the new technology. It is to be an economic unit, a way of life, as well as a political entity. A model constitution drawn up by government technicians is available to the new villages to adapt to their own conditions.

The philosophy underlying the *Ujamaa* village programme is both interesting and attractive. These are its main features:

(a) Modern technology, increased production, and the increased incomes made possible by the new technology are desirable; but a system of organization is needed which will avoid the great inequalities likely to occur if modernization is left solely to market forces and private decisions guided by the profit motive.

(b) People must be concentrated locationally so that it is easier to provide services and upgrade the skills needed for a modern agriculture – services such as education, health, technical assistance, marketing and credit. Such concentration is also deemed advantageous for the establishment of small industries in rural areas. Likewise, it is important for developing political consciousness and loyalty to a nation state.

(c) Villagization with its equalization of opportunities and the creation of new ones is expected to reduce rural-to-urban migration which is occurring at an accelerated rate.

(d) An ideological component is also evident – a faith in living and working together and in sharing with one's neighbours.

This policy introduces two basic changes not part of the

traditional system: the physical movement of residence required by large numbers of people (this of course can occur gradually over time), and the communal operation of economic enterprises. The traditional system was based on individual operation, although there had always been a great deal of informal community cooperation among individual farmers, as is true of peasant communities everywhere.

This policy is without sufficient experience (both geographically and temporally) to predict how it may eventually evolve. Very little research has been done which could provide more details for an evaluation. Likewise, policy lines are not clear with respect to: the rate at which the policy will be implemented; the extent to which farmers will be able to retain a private parcel for their individual use; whether other forms of tenure will be allowed to exist side by side and compete with *Ujamaa* village settlements, etc. Tanzania's policy, however, is illustrative of the general open and experimental attitude which prevails in many of the African nations as they attempt to deal with the developmental problems posed by their traditional land tenure structures.

Dahomey offers still another interesting variation of group farming called rural development cooperatives. This programme, begun in the early 1960s, had nearly forty of these cooperatives in operation in 1971. These cooperatives are located mostly in areas of oil palm production, but some also produce rice and other crops. Their management councils consist of six elected members plus three government officials who hold veto power over certain production and marketing decisions. The establishment of these rural development cooperatives involves several stages:

(a) A detailed land survey and title registration clarifies present ownership status. Substantial areas covered by the cooperatives were claimed by individuals in some form of locally recognized private property. There is opportunity for appeal to a judicial body before these title claims are finalized.

(b) All land is then organized and operated in a collective system, but individuals retain title to an identifiable area of land. This land cannot be withdrawn from the cooperative, but it does revert to the claimant for private operation should the scheme fail.

(c) Owners are issued shares in proportion to the land they bring into the cooperative, and the shares draw an annual interest payment.

(d) Work teams with various specialized tasks are organized, and daily labour records are kept for everyone participating in the farm work. Differential wages are paid, depending on the skill requirements of the tasks performed.

(e) After a specified number of full labour days on the cooperative enterprise, a share is issued to the labourer which is equivalent in value to a share issued for a unit of land contributed. These shares likewise draw an annual interest payment. Those with initial advantages as a result of having more land tend to lose this advantage as the labour shares form a greater proportion of the total. If a person chooses not to work he simply draws the interest due him on his accumulated shares. If he works, he is of course paid wages in addition to his interest and can accumulate additional shares.

(f) Private plots, mainly for subsistence food crops, are farmed on a common rotation basis somewhat along the lines followed by the Egyptian cooperatives. All private plots are contiguous, and the layout is such that certain operations can be performed on a multi-unit basis. The produce from the private plots is left to the use and control of the individual family.

Several of the larger cooperatives have been combined to form a super-cooperative with central facilities for certain capital, equipment, processing and marketing functions. This experiment in Dahomey is impressive and certainly appears to be succeeding. Its general outlines correspond to attempts, introduced in some other French overseas areas, to adapt tenure and production structures to meet the specific needs of certain crops (FAO Report, 1971).

With the exception of the large estates existing in some areas of Eastern Europe, most of the examples of post-reform reorganization discussed to this point have been in areas where, although ownership units may have been large, farming operations were carried out on relatively small units, often through a system of sharecropping and tenancy. If the post-reform organization desired is a family-farm system of peasant farms, the task of reform is essentially one of severing the ties that bind the tenant to the landlord, since farming is already carried out in small units. In addition to the transfer of ownership to former tenants, restructuring of credit and marketing channels must accompany such reforms otherwise, even though land ownership has changed, the new owners may continue to be dependent on the former landlords.

Different issues arise, however, if the pre-reform system consists of large estates operated as large units with hired labour (or, as in parts of Latin America, with permanent labour having various ties to the large estate). Infrastructure, such as farm buildings and irrigation systems, as well as field layouts and the type of machinery, are designed for large unit operation. The options for post-reform reorganization are different in systems starting from a base of small operating units than in those starting with large estate operating units. Given existing infrastructural investments and farm layouts, it is often very costly to split these large estates into family-farm units. Also, in many cases the reform beneficiaries will not have had the managerial experience common to farmers who have managed farms under a small farm tenancy system.

Thus, in reforming a large estate system, additional questions arise: What size and type of units are to be created? Who shall be the beneficiaries and how shall they be selected? If only the permanent workers associated with the estate are to share the land, they may become a new privileged class. Some means must be found to incorporate the landless, seasonal workers, and those owning tiny parcels. These issues greatly complicate the implementation of reform. An illustration of how they have been addressed in at least one case is provided by Chile's land reform.

Under the Chilean agrarian reform, the expropriated large estate is converted into a cooperatively worked *asentamiento* (or settlement). There is usually a time lag between expropriation and the final organization of an *asentamiento*, and at times several expropriated properties are combined into one cooperatively organized production unit. For example, by January 1970, 575 *asentamientos* were in operation, but these held only about two thirds of the total amount of land which had been expropriated up to that time (Thiesenhusen, 1971a). Expropriations have accelerated considerably under the Allende government which took office in November 1970.

On the usual *asentamiento* the physical layout of the former large estate is not changed. Work is accomplished by specialized crews attending specific enterprises. The settler selection process usually gives preference to former permanent workers on the expropriated estate, but others can be included if they have experience as agricultural workers, renters, or sharecroppers; do not own a parcel of land larger than an 'economic unit' as defined in Chilean law; and are over eighteen years of age and head of a family.

Settlers elect a five-member committee, and this committee and CORA (the official agrarian reform agency) contract to formally establish the *asentamiento* organization. An administrative council, composed of the five-member settlement committee and usually several members of CORA's staff, draws up farm production plans which are later formalized in a general assembly of all peasants (*campesinos*) on the property. Settlers agree to live on the farm, carry a share of the work, not cede their rights to others, and market all cooperatively grown produce through official cooperative channels (those crops grown individually on each member's private plot, and privately owned animals for which each member is granted some free grazing rights, are exempted from this marketing provision). During the year individuals receive cash advances, and at the end of the accounting year the farm's net income is divided in accordance with a formula previously agreed upon. Usually CORA takes from 10 to 20 per cent of the net farm income for administrative expenses leaving 80 to 90 per cent to be divided among the *campesinos* (*asentados*) according to the number of days worked. Monthly advances are of course subtracted in calculating the net income to be distributed (Thiesenhusen, 1971a).

Theoretically, the *asentamiento* is an intermediate step lasting from three to five years after which the settlers decide whether the property is to be divided into individual farms or whether the collective pattern of operation is to be continued. From all indications to date, and especially under the present government, it is doubtful that many will be subdivided into individual farms. An intermediate alternative may become more general – group farming on a large part of the *asentamiento* with some private plots for certain types of production.

Beneficiaries are allowed thirty years to pay their land debt which is based on tax-assessed value of the land plus infrastructural investments and other costs incurred by CORA. Debt instalments are adjusted so that the deflated value of total payments will be less than the original debt. Instalments are readjusted to only 70 per cent of the rise in the consumer price index, and no interest is charged on the first three instalments (Thiesenhusen, 1971a; Meyer, 1970).

Additional examples of the wide variety of experiences in group (cooperative-collective) farming are the Mexican *ejidos*, where land is communally owned and cannot be sold or alienated, although most of the land is operated in individual units; the collective enterprises in Cuba; the production cooperatives being established in Peru; the farming corporations in Iran; and the diverse individual–collective system in Israel with its various types of *moshav* settlements and the almost completely collectivized *kibbutz*. However, the most comprehensive and longest experience with collective farming is that of the major communist countries – the Soviet Union, mainland China, and Eastern Europe.

3. State farms. In addition to private family farming and group farming, state farms have been developed in many countries. In several countries in Africa the state has assumed ownership of some of the land and established state farms – 'as islands in a sea of traditional agriculture based upon customary land tenure arrangements. State farms of this sort have been established in Ghana and by Development Boards in Nigeria' (Parsons, 1971, p. 65).

Many of the state farms in Ghana have ceased to function, and tribal claims have been presented to the government asking for compensation for the lands which they incorporated. State farms have also been established in some of the countries in North Africa, the Near East and Latin America. Some state farms exist in almost all countries, either for the production of certain specialized commodities or for experimental breeding and other scientific purposes. But the most prominent examples remain those of the Soviet Union and the countries of Eastern Europe.

State farms differ from collectives in that the former are state enterprises operated by state appointed managers. Labour on state farms is hired in much the same manner as a factory hires its work force. The management of a state farm seems less complicated and therefore provides a greater opportunity for success for an efficient manager than that of a collective (Schiller, 1971). Collective farms are generally managed by a number of committees. The chairman of the top-level managerial committee of a collective is subject to more demands and must include a greater number of frequently conflicting objectives in the plans of operation for such an enterprise (as will be shown in later chapters).

In Rumania, the state farms were created mainly from large private estates confiscated by the state. The state farm system assures the state some measure of direct control over a certain production base and quantity of agricultural produce, and serves as a model for the agricultural collectives. State farms also help improve the general level of farming in their region by demonstrating the effectiveness of modern farming practices and providing improved seeds and breeding stock to farms in the surrounding areas. As noted above, the organization of state farms seems less complex than that of the collectives. They are state-managed enterprises operating with hired labour with a variety of incentives built into the operating procedures. For example, on one large Rumanian state farm specializing in hog production (producing 150,000 market hogs per year) 'profits' in recent years averaged about 25 per cent of total revenue. Thirty per cent of this is retained by the state farm for internal investment purposes. The remainder is paid to the state, but part of it is returned to the enterprise for incentive payments to its workers if all quantity, quality, and cost of production goals have been met.

Evaluation of family farm and collective systems

Is there any evaluative scale with which to weigh the relative advantages and disadvantages of privately operated family farms against those of cooperative-collectives? One approaches such a question with great reservations. About all that can be done is to list some likely elements of positive and negative performance under each type of organization.

As will be discussed in a later chapter, the frequently used argument of economies of scale should not be given much weight in such an evaluation – especially under the labour-surplus conditions existing in most of the less-industrialized countries. Scale economies, however, may become more relevant considerations in the post-reform reorganization of a large estate system than in the land tenure reforms of a share-cropper-tenancy system (for reasons given earlier). There may be important political reasons for establishing a particular type of system, but these will not enter our present evaluation.

If a reasonably egalitarian system of land distribution in family-sized farms is established, such a system may well tend towards greater inequality over time. This will occur as a result of a variety of influences – differential income and price elasticities of demand for different products during the process of development, locational factors in the movement and concentration of industries in the transformation of an agrarian economy into an industrial economy, differences in entrepreneurial abilities, and as a consequence of the latter, differential access to credit and other services, etc.

All farm operators do not have equal entrepreneurial talents. Some would do better working under the direction and supervision of others. Public services such as research, extension and often formal education are more likely to be geared to favour the more aggressive and those in a position to utilize and take advantage of these services. It is easier and apparently more rewarding (within the existing economic and political framework) to work with the more advanced farmers. Ministries of agriculture the world over, and often experimental stations as well, cater to the 'good farmer'.

In a system with rapidly growing opportunities in non-farm

employment, and with the less well-to-do farmers widely dispersed, it is reasonable to expect that such farmers' children, if not they themselves, will be able to advance socially and economically. However, if such new opportunities are not plentiful, or if the disadvantaged are heavily concentrated so that the local public services – especially education and health – are poorly financed, then inequalities are likely to grow and accumulate from generation to generation until such time as special policy measures are introduced to reverse the trend. On the other hand, if measures for the preservation of equality place restrictions on competition in the markets, resources may be poorly allocated and inefficiently used, and much of the entrepreneurial talent that would surface and develop without these restrictions will not emerge.

However, it is also necessary to recognize the productive and the labour-absorptive capacity inherent in a small-farm system. Under conditions of population pressure on the land and the need to absorb more people in agriculture until such time as farm populations decline in absolute numbers, there is some advantage to a small-farm system in the early stages of industrialization. Later, when industry is capable of greater labour absorption and the farm population stabilizes, the inequalities likely to develop in the farm sector as a result of the forces noted above can more easily be dealt with.

A collective system does not assure that a reasonable degree of equality will be maintained. However, both a small farm system based on private property in land as well as a collective system offer the possibility of reducing significantly the great inequalities existing in many of the less-developed countries today. A collective system may provide some additional protection against the reoccurrence of inequalities which are likely to emerge in a system with private property and family farms. However, maintaining a relatively egalitarian system is dependent on the nature of policies in other areas as well – taxation, education, industrial location, etc.

The collective system also faces certain difficulties. Decision making may be much more complex. Since farming is concerned with biological and natural processes, constant judgement and the ability to make on-the-spot decisions and take the necessary action is required. Furthermore, while decisions on a larger scale may be advantageous for the rapid introduction of new technology, a mistake in judgement may be much more costly. The greater the centralization, the greater this danger and the more difficult it may be to detect and correct such errors. Also, collective operations may tend to suppress, or make more difficult, the emergence of the existing and potential entrepreneurial talents. Finally, the task of creating sufficient incentives is a difficult one. There is little comfort in the romantic notion that people will happily work together and share willingly with others the fruits of their labour. There is always reason to doubt whether or not others are carrying their share of the work.

None of the consequences of either system is inevitable or ordained by natural law. The above discussion points to some of the key economic variables (there are others, and political and social considerations as well) that must be weighed if and when opportunities arise which permit the implementation of fundamental changes in a country's land tenure structure.

A land tenure system, however, is not chosen on grounds of economic efficiency and productivity alone. Post-reform land tenure reorganization questions are of a different order and kind than those involved in choosing the location or design of a highway or shopping around for the best deal in the purchase of industrial equipment for the establishment of a steel mill. The former (land tenure) questions are subject to more complex and compelling tests.

A system of state and economy depends upon institutions which constitute a set of human relationships held together by widely accepted procedures and working rules. Changes affecting these procedures are subject to what may be called a constitutional test – how does the new rule or procedure (the land tenure arrangements being evaluated) fit into the existing system of rules – the philosophical, ideological paradigm on which the system is based?

The constitutional criteria will require answers to questions such as the following: What implications does the decollectivization of agriculture and the adoption of a farming system based on private property have for the general principle of establishing a socialist state? Or, what does confiscation of land for reform purposes imply for the maintenance of a system based on private property and a market economy?

It is quite evident that decisions concerning the post-reform organization in agriculture are not based solely on criteria of economic efficiency. These decisions are intimately related to the larger questions of political philosophy and ideology.

Limitations of land reform

Land reform alone, no matter how sweeping, cannot effectively deal with the multitude of issues involved in development. As the land tenure system is reformed, providing a better distribution of land resources and security on the land for the individuals and groups involved, a wide range of other programmes must be intensified and/or modified in order to best serve the new system. Infrastructural investments may be required, credit institutions may need to be created or their policies reshaped to serve a new clientele, the marketing system and its channels must be made consistent with the new tenure structure, and new technologies must be made available and credit and technical assistance provided to facilitate their adoption. In Mosher's terms, 'a progressive rural structure' must be created (Mosher, 1969).

In many countries, agrarian reform remains an *ad hoc* activity. The major objectives of the reform agency are not integrated and incorporated into the working and controlling philosophies of the traditional agencies and ministries. These established agencies often retain their pre-reform objectives and working procedures and set their priorities accordingly. Yet their objectives may be at cross purposes with those of the land reform agency. Even though the agrarian reform agency may have authority to duplicate certain functions of these traditional bodies, it remains in competition with them for funds and personnel. Therefore, far-reaching changes in the governmental sector must often accompany land reform, and changes in the private sectors (or auxiliary public sectors as the case may be – marketing, banking, processing, etc.) must be equally far-reaching.

Since our fundamental concern in this chapter has been with land reform in its narrower meaning of tenure reform, we have not elaborated on these broader issues. However, attention is due these other measures since the success or failure of tenure reforms will hinge on the additional adjustments made in the overall structures serving agriculture.

In the three chapters to follow, land reform will be evaluated in terms of several developmental consequences – distribution, employment and productivity. The usual procedure will be to outline the theoretical connections between land reform and the specific consequence in question, followed by empirical evidence from case illustrations for pre-reform and post-reform experience.

3 Realignments of Power and Income Through Land Reform

Since human relationships include elements of both conflict and interdependence, complex institutional systems are part and parcel of all associated living. Without such systems there is chaos, and relations among men revert to the Hobbesian condition of war of all against all where 'the life of man is solitary, poor, nasty, brutish, and short'. Institutions govern the economic, social and political power relations between individuals and groups, and affect directly their interdependence as well as the achievement of reasonable order from the ever-present and potential conflicts growing out of these relations.

In the process of modernization, with the introduction of technology, increased specialization and productivity, and expanded opportunities for participation in a commercial, exchange-oriented economy, institutions also change. Indeed they must change to permit the incorporation of new ideas, new techniques, and new modes of organization. These are interacting phenomena with new production processes placing pressure on existing institutions and institutional change altering the directions of development.

Identifying the specific consequences of basic institutional change is complicated by many unintended and often unobserved side effects. New directions in policy set in motion changes which come to influence on their own the future course of events in a society. In historical perspective, however, the influence of land tenure institutions (and their change) on the basic power relations in society are more easily identified. In the following analysis, therefore, we shall look at these processes from several historical points of view.

The sources of power

In agrarian societies, before the widespread use of capital and industrial production techniques, those who control the use of land also control the economic, social and political levers of power. Until several centuries ago, there is little question but that power in all societies was associated with the ownership or control of land. 'The comparative wealth, esteem, military position and the sanguinary authority over the lives of the populace that went with landownership assured its possessor of a position of eminence in his community and power in the state' (Galbraith, 1967, p. 51).

With the industrial revolution, different factors of production took on primary importance and capital became the most limiting factor. Consequently, power over an enterprise, 'and by derivation in the society at large', passed to those who had control over capital. 'And so did prestige in the community and authority in the state' (Galbraith, 1967, p. 55).

In modern industrial societies, with large complex corporations, governments and other forms of human organization, concern over the control of farm land as a major social issue is greatly reduced. Certainly if an individual or a group controls the necessary capital, land can always be obtained; but even control over land and capital is insufficient. A new ingredient in the modern production process has become a critical factor in determining success (in large business enterprises as well as in large organizations generally). This new element, which Galbraith calls the 'technostructure', is the integrated highly specialized technical knowledge contributed by all those who process and analyse information which is incorporated into group decisions in large organizations.

This changing significance of control over the several basic factors of production during the process of development provides a clue as to the influence of the land tenure system on the economic, social and political power relations in an agrarian society. This can be shown by contrasting the land tenure system in a highly industrialized nation and that common to a traditional, agrarian society (see Kanel, 1971).

Land tenure in an industrial society

In the United States, for example, land tenure arrangements function primarily to provide flexibility and to supplement the assets of farm operators. Tenancy has become largely an economic mechanism for capital mobility with relatively little social or political significance.[1] Both land tenure and credit institutions serve to provide flexibility in reorganizing farm firms to accommodate factor availabilities and factor costs as these change in response to changing technology. Land and capital per worker have increased as labour has become more expensive.

The situation within every tenure group is affected by the availability of and access to alternatives. So long as economic development continues to expand opportunities and improve incomes in alternative employments, the power of one party over the other in a landlord–tenant relation is limited. Incomes earned by either party are influenced more by the relatively impersonal conditions in factor markets than by the personal ability of one party to dominate the other. Landlords, an occupationally diverse group, find few common interests related specifically to their ownership of farm land. A bad relationship between a landlord and tenant can result in financial loss to either or both parties, but it is the individual landlord or tenant (rather than landlords or tenants as a class) who will be viewed as the enemy. The basic characteristics of the land tenure system in this setting are lack of group interests and absence of class oppression along tenure lines. These characteristics are brought about largely by the opportunity structure and the economic and social mobility which it provides (Kanel, 1971).

In such a system, the tenure status of a farm family may change a number of times throughout its lifetime. Young families may rent land and become tenants; tenants buy land and become owners; full-owners rent additional land and become part-owners; some small farms are combined into larger ones while others continue to be operated as independent units.

1. This has not always been the case, especially in the U S South. Even here, however, the situation is rapidly changing.

Additionally, farm people may have investments and hold jobs in the non-farm sector. The major point is that the reorganization of US agriculture toward larger farms using more capital and less labour and achieving higher family incomes has affected the entire range of tenure classes. Changes in farm size and in the factor proportions used in farming have been made by owners and part-owners as well as by tenants.

US farmers have created – frequently along commodity lines – marketing, supply and bargaining cooperatives, as well as highly potent political organizations active in areas such as: control over monopoly power in farm factor and product markets, farm price policy, regulation of imports, export promotion and subsidization, and federal aid for local services such as research, education, conservation, credit, and roads. Farmers in the United States have not organized along land tenure lines in more than a century. Such organization along tenure lines did exist in the early years preceding and immediately following the American Revolution, and it was central to the divided – half slave, half free – farm economy before the Civil War. However, once the United States (as industrial countries generally) completed the task of transforming feudal-like institutions, organization was along lines other than land tenure.

Land tenure in a traditional society

The role of land tenure institutions under present US conditions is in sharp contrast to that in the institutional structure of traditional societies. A traditional society is defined as one where product markets are not highly developed and where there is almost complete absence of markets for land and labour. In this sense, there is no traditional society anywhere corresponding to an entire nation state. There are, however, regions and isolated areas within many of the less developed countries where such traditional societies continue to exist.

In traditional societies, a person's station in life and his occupation are not determined by bargains freely entered into but are the result primarily of an inherited status. Tenure rules provide access to a piece of land and often include an obligation to pass on some of the produce or to work for a social superior.

Under the Anglo-American legal system, an owner of fee-simple title can operate the land himself, he can sell it, or he can bring in a tenant under terms established by contract between him and the tenant. Such an owner can eliminate the existing relationships between himself and others connected with his land and establish new ones. By way of contrast, such a right 'to wipe the slate clean' does not exist in traditional societies. The whole structure, with various people having customary commitments and obligations to each other, is such that no person within that system has a clear right to abolish one set of relationships and to bring in people as workers or tenants on a new set of terms. In that sense there is neither a market for land nor for labour (Kanel, 1971).

Economic alternatives which would temper possible abuses by the upper rural classes are absent; there is little security against unfairness and whims of those above. On the other hand, there is much greater security and stability of occupations due to the absence of change in production techniques and the fixity of class lines. There is much less instability equivalent to that generated in modern times by changing technology and economic forces which change market conditions and decisions made by employers. In relation to the peasants, those with superior class status combine, in an undifferentiated manner, social and political leadership with their economic roles (in modern societies such leadership roles are distributed among government officials, officials of interest groups, community leaders, and others).

The capitalist or the entrepreneur has not yet emerged in such a society. The self-image of upper classes is likely to include the assumption of a right to leadership, superior status, and services from the peasants combined with certain obligations to those below. The manipulable social situations include intrigues and combinations with peers and others of higher status, and tightening or loosening control over peasants along with the granting of favours. This self-image does not include an impersonal view of peasants or those in lower classes as outsiders with whom one has no relations except as one chooses to contract with them for work or services. This is not because such impersonal relations with a labour force are rejected as dishonourable; it is simply because the possibility and recognition of such a relation emerges only gradually out of the interrelated changes in technology, production organization, and the development of national markets and institutions (Kanel, 1971).

The relationship between upper and lower classes in traditional societies is not necessarily one of despotic use of power by those above. It may be a beneficial and mutually supporting arrangement between lord (or chief) and peasant. Rights and duties become institutionalized, honoured, and respected. Where a 'law and order' nation state has not yet emerged to come to the aid and service of the more powerful, the upper classes must seek accommodation with those in lower status because they are so greatly outnumbered and because they need the lower classes to help form a common defence against outsiders. And of course, the lower classes need and depend upon those in superior positions for their rights, for assistance, for contact with the outside world, and for the maintenance of order and the resolution of conflicts.

Land tenure in a transitional society

The contrast between traditional arrangements and those that emerge in a modernizing society can be viewed as a contrast between a relatively stable technology and social order on the one hand, and a changing technology and a more fluid social order on the other. The valuable rights of the upper classes in traditional society stem from superior status in the social organization rather than from ownership of land as such. But in the process of modernization, attitudes toward land and labour change and land *per se* becomes valuable. Those in superior positions may claim exclusive rights to land, i.e. a conception of land as a commodity emerges over which exclusive ownership must be secured. The idea gradually emerges that an 'owner' can cultivate the land with tenants or hired workers and establish the social order *on his land* by his choice of terms of labour and tenure arrangements. Since the upper classes in the traditional setting are able to take advantage of new technology by virtue of their superior status, their power position is enhanced. Technology thus introduces changes that alter the structure of opportunities and as a consequence the former relations and mutual dependencies are also altered (Kanel, 1971).

The process of modernization provides a strong incentive to move toward greater individual rights and abrogation of group controls. Where the upper class assumes the initiative in exploiting the gains inherent in the new technology, it develops an interest in freeing itself of obligations to the peasants and in gaining full control over land. There is a shift from the aristocratic tradition to a capitalist outlook recognizing the benefits from technological and economic opportunities which can be realized only as the power of the state is used to protect private property and the enforcement of contracts. For this and other reasons, modernization strengthens the authority of central state power. Whenever the upper rural classes become actively engaged in management they will seek to shed social obligations, gain a free hand in controlling land use, and obtain the services of a 'law-and-order' state in protecting their property (Kanel, 1971).

Where modernization takes the form of the emergence of a land-owning peasantry, the peasants seek to eliminate the land rights of both the upper classes as well as those of the peasant community. Attempts to remove the rights of the upper classes stem from peasant desires for security, from loss of traditional functions of the upper classes, or from shifts in political power of the landed upper classes *vis-á-vis* the peasantry. The freedom from community controls finds its rationale in the possibility of individual adoption of technology, the prospect of using credit on the security of their landownership, and the need to free individual innovators from group claims to their gains.

Agrarian transformations and their political consequences

Historically, it is possible to identify several different courses by which agrarian systems have been transformed. In all cases of the developed, industrialized nations, a crucial step toward the modern world has been 'separating a large section of the ruling class from direct ties with the land, a separation that has taken place sooner or later in every industrialized country'

(Moore, 1966, p. 279). Moore identifies three major routes from the pre-industrial to the modern world.

The first of these he refers to as the bourgeois revolutions, representing the

> violent changes that took place in English, French and American societies on the way to becoming modern industrial democracies and that historians connect with the Puritan Revolution (or the English Civil War as it is often called as well), the French Revolution, and the American Civil War. . . . The landed upper classes, our main concern at the start, were either an important part of this capitalist and democratic tide, as in England, or if they opposed it, they were swept aside in the convulsions of revolution or civil war. The same thing may be said about the peasants. Either the main thrust of their political efforts coincided with that toward capitalism and political democracy, or else it was negligible (Moore, 1966, p. xv).

This first route, then, led to the combination of capitalism and Western democracy.

A second route was also capitalist, but culminated during the twentieth century in fascism as in Germany and Japan. Moore calls this 'the capitalist and reactionary form.'

> It amounts to a form of revolution from above. . . sections of a relatively weak commercial and industrial class relied on dissident elements in the older and still dominant ruling classes, mainly recruited from the land, to put through the political and economic changes required for a modern industrial society, under the auspices of a semi-parliamentary regime. But the outcome, after a brief and unstable period of democracy, has been fascism (pp. xv and xvi).

The third route identified by Moore is communism as exemplified by Russia and China.

> The great agrarian bureaucracies of these countries served to inhibit the commercial and later industrial impulses even more than in the preceding instances. The results were two fold. In the first place these urban classes were too weak to constitute even a junior partner in the form of modernization taken in Germany and Japan, though there were attempts in this direction. And in the absence of more than the most feeble steps toward modernization a huge peasantry remained. This stratum, subject to new strains and stresses as the modern world encroached upon it, provided the main destructive revolutionary force that overthrew the old order and propelled

these countries into the modern era under communist leadership that made the peasants its primary victims (p. xvi).

Moore's broad historical analysis suggests that the methods by which land tenure institutions are changed have a direct influence on the resulting socio-political and economic systems. The whole array of agrarian-based patterns of living, structures of authority, and all the supporting, traditional and accepted ways of rural life are basically altered in the process. His detailed case studies support the following two propositions:

1. The economic, social and political power relations of the pre-industrial agrarian system are inconsistent with the requirements of an industrial society.

2. The way in which the agrarian structure is changed has an important bearing on the resulting institutional system.

In highly industrialized countries, the land tenure system has lost much of its social and political significance and functions primarily as an economic instrument. The change from a tenure system where social and political aspects are dominant features to one where the social and political attributes have become separated defines the general process of institutional transformation.

Kanel's analysis, summarized above, deals with the emergence of the modern state in a historical setting most nearly representing Moore's first route – the bourgeois revolutions culminating in capitalism and political democracy. Kanel identifies four transitional stages:

1. Where the state is weak (or non-existent) in relation to the rural upper class.

2. To a stage where the rural elite needs and uses the state.

3. To a further stage where the rural elite's leadership and power over the peasants is challenged by other contenders.

4. To a modern stage where farm people and other interest groups build up organizations (pressure or lobbying groups) responsive to their needs and effective in influencing government policy.

The second stage corresponds to landlord dominance of local

politics, the third to political pressure on the landlord class and demands for land reform, and the last to a tenure system stripped of political and social significance similar to tenure in the US described earlier (Kanel, 1971).

Land reform is a major disruptive, yet usually creative, force in the life of a people. A nation that is to develop may not be able to escape it. Conceivably, industry might grow fast enough to provide sufficient alternative employment opportunities, enabling new groups to achieve higher status outside of agriculture, thereby decreasing the relative power of the landowning groups. Experience to date, however, does not warrant optimism for this possibility. Perhaps the big landowners can carry out the modernization process following the pattern of the landed elite in Britain. However, Britain was the first country to industrialize and generated its own technology internally. It also had a much slower population growth than do the less-developed nations today.

Pressures for land reform do not generally emerge in a traditional society, but rather in one undergoing change and transition. New technology, market opportunities, new consumer products – these lead men to doubt the efficacy of traditional arrangements, transform land from a commonly shared subsistence base into a resource with commercial value, and lead to changed attitudes concerning labour and mutual obligations. Those in positions of power in the traditional setting are best able to take advantage of the new possibilities, obtain legally sanctioned ownership or otherwise consolidate their control over land resources, and reap the major benefits from increased productivity. In the process, the gulf between rich and poor widens – in terms of economic and political power, social status, income, education and culture.

Thus land reform involves more than modification at the margins; it consists of profound changes in power patterns via changes in the distribution of resources and income-earning opportunities. Land is expropriated or confiscated and redistributed in order to achieve this. Wherever land reform has been successfully implemented, the basic thrust has been to break the political and economic power of the landlords.

In that transitional stage in the movement from a traditional to an industrial society, those who control the land resources are able to influence the political processes in a measure disproportionate to their numbers, and their influence largely shapes the goals and policies that are formulated through such processes. In fact, the rural poor frequently view the national government with apprehension and seek to avoid its attention rather than to influence it for their own purpose. As a consequence, it is extremely difficult to enact legislation affecting the distribution of income – whether by land tenure changes or by other means. If such legislation is passed, it is difficult to enforce. Taxes are usually low, the system of taxation confused, and compliance minimal. The same problems exist with enforcement of laws governing rural working conditions or land rental contracts.

Power at the national level is likely to be closely associated with power at the regional and local levels. Even if a local group outside this power structure formulates and pressures for a certain programme, it may be confronted by opposition from the local power elite and may likewise find this same opposition at the regional and central levels because common interests are involved. Under these circumstances, people remain either politically inactive or they revolt. The prospect of an intermediate alternative – compromise and negotiation – is largely foreclosed.

In the abstract, it may seem reasonable to argue that changes in the distribution of income and the distribution of political power have analogous possibilities. That is to say, a highly skewed pattern of income distribution may result in a lower level of effective demand and consequently in a lower level of total national income. Under conditions of mass unemployment and under-utilization of resources, a more equal distribution stimulates demand, given time for the multiplier effect to register its full impact, thus enlarging the total income 'pie'. By analogy one may suggest that the same applies to political power – a wider distribution may in the long run enhance the power of all.

The length of run and the dynamics of the particular situation are, of course, important variables. In a rapidly growing economy, the generation of new wealth and power may be sufficient to provide growing opportunities for all interest groups over time. However, since this cannot be guaranteed, even in the long run, those who stand to lose in the short run will not voluntarily take this risk. They may have to accept the risk if there is sufficient diffusion of power among many interests. But the more agrarian a transitional system, the more highly is this power likely to be concentrated in the hands of a few and the greater is the influence of the associated land tenure system. This influence recedes as industrialization advances and as groups other than those favoured by the landholding system gain a larger share of the income and power.

Access routes to future income

Although increased productivity is a requisite of economic development, there is no direct or necessary connection between increased productivity and a greater equality in its distribution: the benefits from increased output and increased efficiency may accrue to a very small group within the population. Unless the access routes to income via tenure relationships are altered and made more secure, there is no automatic assurance that the distributional problem will diminish.

Access to the future stream of income in any society has two dimensions: (a) the initial access route, and (b) the continued security of such access. Initial access to the potential income stream takes many forms. In many countries, a basic means is private (individual or group) ownership of resources. Except in a slave or semi-slave society, every person owns and controls his labour time and may contract its use to secure some access to income. But if those who own or otherwise control the need for complementary resources (required to make this labour productive of economic goods and services) do not offer to contract for this labour time, the mere ownership of one's labour does not assure access to the future productivity of that society. If a person owns other resources in addition to his labour (land, or capital, or useful intellectual or manual skills), he can be more confident of gaining access to the future income flow.

People use other means than ownership to gain access to the annual production of a society. Credit can be used to acquire present use of a resource in which ownership is secured in the future. Resources can be rented. Governments may guarantee individuals an access to income through unemployment compensation, social security payments, educational subsidies, scholarships, and direct employment in government owned enterprises.

All the above give some initial access to income. Such initial access may provide a large or a small pipeline into the income stream. Likewise, the pipeline may be firmly welded or may have only a very loose, tenuous connection. A person who has only his labour to sell (to the management of a large corporation or to a large landowner) has little power to secure a firm hold on future productivity. To increase the security of access to the income stream, as well as to increase their individual incomes, labourers have formed unions and so increased their bargaining power *vis-à-vis* employers (Dorner, 1964).

Rural and urban differences

The responses of peasants and that of industrial workers in trying to gain access and security to the future income stream which the economy produces are quite different. Conditions in the two sectors – agricultural and industrial – are not comparable (Kanel, 1971). Individual ownership of the means of production in industry is an impractical goal because of the decisive economies of scale in modern industry. Thus, workers have increased their economic power by unionization and by lobbying for legislation requiring collective bargaining and the establishment of procedures to handle grievances and to govern dismissal of workers. Protection against unemployment and low-income employment is increased by state action such as expansionary fiscal and monetary policies, minimum wage legislation, and public unemployment insurance.

For several reasons, it is easier to build security and flexibility into industrial employment. Large numbers of workers within one establishment make it easier for them to organize and identify common interests. They may even be able to maintain wages substantially above the market rate and deny employment to those outside. Alleviation of the problems of those excluded is not viewed as their responsibility. Industrial workers usually do not live in company-owned housing. If the urban area is relatively large, they are likely to live near a number of potential employers. In sum, urban conditions, especially if industrial development proceeds at a rapid pace, are more conducive to changes in place of employment and to a more impersonal relationship between employers and workers (Kanel, 1971).

Rural conditions are quite different in all these respects. In most types of farming, there are no decisive economies of scale so that family and large farms can coexist. Development is less likely to increase the demand for labour in farming than in industry, and in a farm sector dominated by large landholdings modernization may even decrease employment opportunities. Development is often much more disruptive in agriculture since it involves changes in a pre-existing structure, whereas industrial expansion is more in the nature of establishing new activities (or out-competing and displacing the existing craft and cottage industries) without an old structure to modify. In many types of large-scale agriculture, workers live on the farms of their employers. Loss of job means loss of home and home community, and potential alternative employers are more distant than in urban areas. Farm workers who live in homes of their own are usually hired on large farms by the day, working at seasonal tasks only when work requirements exceed the capacity of a farm's resident labour force. Employment available to such temporary workers is usually the most insecure, and they are often the most poverty stricken of all rural classes.

For all these reasons, peasants have not been able to utilize as well the protective devices of industrial workers. An exception is the unionization of some plantation workers, reflecting the fact that a plantation is often more like a factory than like a farm. The peasant remedy more typically has been the drive to achieve land ownership and to supplement this with public and cooperative service organizations.[2] These are his means of

2. This is why any revolution 'from above', imposing a tenure system other than that of small farms of an independent peasantry, usually requires a certain amount of coercion. A revolution 'from below', with the peasants in charge, will seek to establish individualized private property in land. This has been true throughout modern history.

assuring initial access and the security of a growing income over time.

Security of access to future income does not mean a guarantee in a particular occupation. Changing circumstances modify the conditions and security of access to income. A small farmer with good initial access to income via ownership may lose his security of future access if he fails to keep up with new production techniques. Or, people may, through incompetence or lack of effort, sacrifice their access and security of access to future income. The critical need is for the creation of sufficient alternatives and the human capacities needed to exploit them so that people can regain access to opportunities.

In addition to the equity, welfare and social justice considerations implicit in income redistribution measures, there are other development purposes to be served by such redistributions. The one of major economic significance is the consequence of increased rural incomes on the expansion of demand for manufactured consumer goods, for manufactured farm inputs, and for farm-produced output.

Issues in income redistribution

Clearly, a more equal distribution of income does not mean complete equality – a goal that would be near impossible even if it were desired. Also, substantial improvement in peasant incomes is a long, slow process. In less-developed countries, the majority of the population is very poor, and most of the poor are peasants (Owen, 1966). Even complete equality in the distribution of national incomes would not significantly raise the incomes for all these rural poor. Redistribution of incomes – in the context of the present discussion, a redistribution of income-earning opportunities through land reform – must be accompanied by increased productivity and a dynamic rate of growth in output, or it will simply result in a levelling of income downward – a temporary benefit for the poor at best. Dovring (1962) comments:

In a land redistribution program, it is desirable to increase the 'distributive equity' in the community, and at the same time raise agricultural productivity. The former may be clearly desirable if the existing distribution of landed wealth is extremely unequal, including a few very rich and a mass of very poor people. There is empirical evidence, e.g. from the Mediterranean countries, to show that such an extreme distribution often acts as a bottleneck to development because it may deprive both the very rich and the very poor of any real incentive to work for higher productivity. . . . subdivision of large holdings into small ones is often favorable to total net factor productivity (in the country as a whole) when external capital is scarce (p. 33).

It is sometimes argued that concentration of income and wealth is required for a high savings rate and thus for high rates of investment and capital formation. However, most evidence on this question tends to support the opposite conclusion. The under-development of some of the petroleum and mineral-rich countries, where wealth is often highly concentrated, is a case in point (Long, 1964). The Economic Commission for Latin America (ECLA) has compiled evidence showing that there is no close statistical correlation between a high degree of income concentration and national development.

ECLA's comparisons show that in Latin America average incomes of the top 5 per cent are 20 times greater than average incomes of the lower 50 per cent of income earners. In Europe this difference is only half as great while in the United States it is even less (Thiesenhusen, 1970, p. 7; ECLA, 1968, p. 50).

Kaldor's (1959) evaluation of the Chilean situation also bears on this point. He concluded that there was a substantial savings potential that could be realized if the luxury consumption of property owners could be reduced to a more modest proportion of their income. He maintains further that the proportion of savings in the national income could be raised considerably without lowering the standard of living of the mass of the population. Dovring (1962) arrives at a similar conclusion:

In both Western Europe and Japan, the landlord class was sufficiently entrepreneur-minded to use its rents (or at least a large share of them) for capital formation. The real disadvantage about agricultural rents in underdeveloped countries is not so much that they are high, but rather that they are too often used up for luxury consumption and too seldom invested in new productive ventures. Especially when the luxuries have a high import content, or rely to a high degree on traditional handicrafts and service occupations in the home country, they largely fail to set off progressive capital accumulation (p. 37).

Actually, then, savings propensities are very low in precisely the countries where income distribution is the most unequal.[3] The industrialized nations, with a more equal distribution of income, have the higher savings ratios. It is of course true that savings are a direct function of the level of family income, but part of the explanation at least must lie in the high consumption levels of the wealthy.

In a society with 50 per cent or more of its population dependent on agriculture (a common feature of less-developed countries), the income level of this majority is a key factor in determining the demand for goods and services in the economy. When most people are poor, desperately poor, very little demand is generated. This applies to the demand for agricultural products themselves. If the income generated from the production of farm products is highly concentrated among a relatively small group, people may be starving amidst the accumulation of surpluses. Poor people are poor customers; they would eat more and eat better if they had more income.

A number of studies conducted in Latin America indicate the magnitude of the inequalities in the agricultural sectors of some countries in that region. In the early 1960s, the upper 3 per cent of the agricultural population in Chile received over 35 per cent of the agricultural income while the lower-income 70 per cent received only one-third (Barraclough and Domike, 1966, p. 405). In the Central American countries, over 80 per cent of the families in agriculture have family incomes of less than $1000 per year (most of them much less than this) while the top 5 per cent of families in agriculture have family incomes from ten to thirty times higher than those in the lower-income strata (Quiros, 1971, p. 148).

It may be impossible to sustain industrial (and even agricultural) output and productivity increases without a more equal distribution of income which generates a wider and a more

3. Additionally there is the tendency for those with high incomes to invest abroad.

effective market demand. Supply does not create its own demand, especially under conditions of a highly skewed income distribution. Under most conditions, separating the policy issues of increasing production and establishing a more equal distribution of income is self-defeating since the distributional measures may be strategic for achieving sustained increases in production (Dorner, 1971a).

One needs to qualify the latter statement. As Dovring has noted, if those who collect the rents and other payments leading to high incomes channel their savings into the appropriate investments, development may occur. However, many of the investments needed simply cannot be made by private entrepreneurs. This is certainly the case for many of the major infrastructural requirements of the country. However, a more basic qualification is that the statement in the preceding paragraph refers to a relatively 'free market' economy. Means other than reliance on the market are available to a centrally planned system. The state may, at least for a time, substitute its demands for those of consumers. Even here, however, a balance between the distribution of purchasing power and production-increasing investments must be maintained.[4]

It may be argued that the increased production of crops and other products for export is not so bound by the insufficient demand resulting from a skewed internal distribution of income. In other words, the expansion of exports can increase foreign exchange earnings with which to import the capital equipment needed for industrialization. This argument is valid to a point, but it depends on how the foreign exchange is used. It too can be dissipated in luxury consumption. Furthermore, much of the production of export crops is developing along fairly capital intensive lines – generating little employment but requiring considerable foreign exchange for its expansion. Over-emphasis on export production has at

4. The absolute size of a country (its population and other resources) becomes an important consideration. Russia was able to concentrate on investments in heavy industry and military hardware for several decades without specific attention to the expansion of consumer demand. Small countries generally do not have the same options, and the expansion of a broadly based consumer demand becomes more critical at an earlier stage in development.

times led to neglect of and a consequent drop in production of subsistence crops, resulting in inflationary pressures or increased imports of food grains. The Central American countries from 1950 to 1968 expanded export crop production but experienced a growing deficit in the production of basic grains.[5] From an exportable surplus of almost 26,000 metric tons of grains annually in the period 1950–54, there was a continuing deterioration with an import of almost 40,000 metric tons annually in the period 1965–68 (Quiros, 1971). 'Although the gains from agricultural production for export have been impressive,' concludes Quiros (1971),

hidden costs need to be evaluated to get an accurate picture of the net gains from export-led agricultural growth. This issue is particularly relevant in the transitional stage of the economic development of Central America, where the extent of the internal market is of paramount importance (p. 140).

Another critical point, of course, is that the prospects for increasing export earnings by expanding agricultural exports are not promising. 'First, the demand for agricultural products is growing slowly in developed countries, and second, the agricultural output of developed countries is growing rapidly, compared with population' (Christensen, 1970, p. 55). The consequences of this situation are quite evident in comparing trade statistics of developed and developing regions over a period of years (Table 1).

The extent of the internal market is indeed of paramount importance for agricultural products; it is of even more critical significance for industrial ones. A lesson from US history has some relevance on this issue. Conrad and Meyer (1964), pp. 228–9) suggest that

slavery [in the US South] produced an income distribution so skewed that it was difficult to support the large mass markets necessary to the development of local consumer-goods production. Seigneurial consumption was not likely to be a substitute for the broad market that could have made it profitable in the South to manufacture consumer goods more sophisticated than the most elemental of subsistence wares.

5. Basic grains include corn, rice, beans and sorghum, according to the Central American Common Market classifications.

This inequality need not have restricted income *growth* in the presence of strong demand pressures in the world cotton markets. However, it is not simply the size but the distribution of income that is crucial for structural change, and it is in respect to the degree of inequality that slavery could have injured the South's early chances for industrialization. Under the burden of this inequality and the consequent inefficiency of manufacturing enterprise, southern industry could not proceed against northern competition (pp. 228–9).

Table 1 Index numbers of total volume of agricultural exports and imports of developing and developed regions, selected years (1957–59 = 100)

Item	1955	1960	1965	1967[1]
Developing regions[2]				
Exports	108	101	112	106
Imports	79	116	141	145
Developed regions[3]				
Exports	91	109	149	153
Imports	90	107	123	128

Notes:
1. Preliminary estimates.
2. Developing regions include Latin America, Far East (excluding Japan and Mainland China), Near East and Africa.
3. Developed regions include Western Europe, North America, Japan and Oceania.
Source: Table 24, p. 55, in Christensen (1970). Source cited by Christensen is Food and Agricultural Organization of the United Nations, 1968, pp. 29 and 35.

Land reform and income redistribution

Many economists agree that a more egalitarian distribution of income can provide a stimulus to demand and subsequent investments – especially in the light consumer-goods industries (Mellor, 1970). Can it be empirically verified that land reform actually leads to a more equal distribution of income? Evidence on pre-reform and post-reform income distribution and expenditure patterns is extremely difficult to obtain. Usually income redistribution must be inferred from statistics showing the redistribution of land.

Under the Egyptian land reform, close to one million acres

of land have been redistributed since the reform began in 1952 (FAO report, 1971). Furthermore, the rent reductions for those continuing as tenants were highly significant in transferring income from the landowning class to the tenant class. The total annual transfer from these two sources has been estimated at over £E40 million annually (Platt, 1970, p. 52).

In Taiwan, the proportion of owner-cultivators increased from 33 per cent of all cultivators in 1948 to 59 per cent in 1959. Adding part-owners to the above gives proportions of 57 and 81 per cent in 1948 and 1959, respectively. The remainder were tenants and farm hands, the combined proportion of which declined from 43 per cent in 1948 to 19 per cent in 1959 (Koo, 1970, p. 40).

Again, especially in the years immediately following the reforms of the late 1940s and early 1950s, the increased income of the cultivators was principally in the form of rent limitations. Later, the gains from complete ownership and increased output represented a larger proportion of the total (Koo, 1970, p. 54). The trend in income distribution in Taiwan's agricultural sector is shown in Table 2.

Bolivia experienced a rapid and revolutionary distributive land reform following its 1952 revolution. There are no national quantitative data to measure changes in income of land reform beneficiaries. However, a number of surveys conducted among reform beneficiaries on Bolivia's high plateau are quite revealing. These surveys attempted to reconstruct expenditure (and barter) patterns of families living on the reformed *haciendas* for the period immediately preceding 1952 and for 1966, the year of the survey. The following figures for a family of five are given in 1966 prices.

Before 1952, the annual value of goods acquired by barter (i.e. the most common, regularly acquired consumption items) equalled US $7·85, and the value of those acquired through cash purchase was $22·80 for a total of $30·65. In 1966, the corresponding figures were $5·05, $95·90, and $100·95. Thus total annual expenditures increased by more than three times while regular participation in the money economy was over four times greater in 1966 than in the pre-1952 period (Clark, 1968, p. 169).

Table 2 Distribution of farm income, Taiwan, 1926-60 (unit: current prices, 1000 T$)

Period	Total agricultural production	Net farm income	Landlords and money lenders	Cultivators	Government and other public institutions
1926-30	297,085	224,809 (100·00)	59,272 (26·37)	149,545 (66·52)	15,992 (7·11)
1936-40	509,014	390,150 (100·00)	98,299 (25·19)	261,707 (67·08)	30,144 (7·73)
1950-55	7,214,976	5,447,963 (100·00)	531,969 (9·76)	4,204,438 (77·18)	711,556 (13·06)
1956-60	16,034,968	11,801,328 (100·00)	738,790 (6·26)	9,609,844 (81·43)	1,452,694 (12·31)

Source: Koo (1970, p. 17); source cited by Koo is Lee (1967, p. 205).

The above expenditures cover only regularly acquired articles. In addition, infrequent purchases of such items as farm tools, implements and work animals (farm capital) and sewing machines, radios and bicycles (consumer durables) were reported to have increased substantially. Clark reports on the changes that took place on one large *hacienda* with approximately 200 families. In 1956, there was only one house with a metal roof and one bicycle; ten years later there were forty metal roofs and eighty bicycles. In the earlier period, there were seven sewing machines and one radio; in the later period, there were 120 sewing machines and 100 radios. In most areas of Bolivia, concludes Clark, the changes have not been this dramatic. But in the northern highlands region, this is not an exceptional case (Clark, 1968, p. 170).

Thiesenhusen studied the reform projects conducted on the lands of the Catholic church in Chile. A unique occasion presented itself for finding out how land-reform beneficiaries budget the additional income they receive. In 1964, the reform beneficiaries on one large farm received a substantial lump-sum final payment from the previous year's operation. Fifteen colonists chosen at random were interviewed two weeks after receiving this payment to find out how it was spent. 'Between the date of the receipt of the cash and the time of our interview, about 41·5 per cent of the average cash available was spent for farm operating expenses and capital. About 39 per cent had been spent for family expenses. Only about 19·5 per cent of the average cash available had been saved' (Thiesenhusen, 1966a, p. 21).[6]

Fragmentary though it is, the evidence from these countries does show that large scale land reforms result in substantial income transfers to the poorer rural classes – the farm workers and cultivators. In those instances where case studies have been made, they show increased participation in the money econ-

6. Thiesenhusen points out that colonists spent quickly upon the receipt of their money because they were aware of how fast inflation depreciates it. Inflation was 38·3 per cent in 1964. 'It does not follow that foolish expenditures are made. Most colonists we interviewed were aware of their capital needs – as they were of their consumption necessities – and made necessary purchases when they received the funds' (Thiesenhusen, 1966a, p. 21).

omy following such income transfers. The new expenditure patterns appeared to be based on economically rational criteria. If a reform is massive and involves a large percentage of the rural people, the new expenditure patterns will change the national structure of demand and the earning rates of capital in alternative uses. There is likely to be a greater stimulus in the simple consumer-goods industries. These industries are more labour intensive in their production processes and also require a lower input of foreign exchange than the industries producing luxury and semi-luxury products for a relatively small group of wealthy landowners (Thiesenhusen, 1970).

Whether or not all these consequences – some obviously undetectable in the short run – actually follow a large-scale reform will depend on government and private action in many other areas – providing yield-increasing inputs, improving roads and transport systems, building up marketing and storage facilities, developing new research and educational capacity, improved credit systems for reaching into the country-side, etc. The point must again be emphasized that land reform does not assure or guarantee all the positive interactions and linkages discussed in this chapter. However, land reform is frequently a necessary condition to provide at least the possibility of inducing and achieving these positive interactions. The prospects of a more egalitarian distribution of income with its subsequent consequences for a changed structure of demand and increased profitability of alternative investments are among the potential benefits of a major land reform.

4 Land Reform and Agricultural Employment

Historically, the agricultural sector has contributed to overall development by releasing workers for employment in industry. But in many countries today, migration from farm to city is proceeding much more rapidly than the growth in urban employment opportunities. Consequently, urban unemployment and underemployment are major problems in most of the developing countries. Under these circumstances, it would be better if more people could be provided with productive opportunities in farming where they might at least produce for their own subsistence.

In seven Latin American countries,[1] data for the decade of the 1950s show that 11 million people of a total natural increase in rural areas of 19 million migrated to the cities. The World Health Organization reports that with present migration trends and with the world population doubling between the late 1960s and the year 2000,

the proportion of urbanized world population will also double – in other words, the city population will increase four fold. . . . today the very shanty-towns of more than 100,000 inhabitants at the fringes of our modern cities concentrate 12 per cent of the world population, more than one-third of the world's city population (quoted by Schumacher, 1966, p. 5).

Urbanization throughout the less-developed world is far ahead of industrialization. In Latin America the 'shantytown-slum' population is estimated 'to be growing at about 15 per cent per year – a rate over 10 percentage points higher than the city population as a whole' (Thiesenhusen, 1969, p. 737). Many of the new entrants into the labour force, of course, remain on the farm as evidenced by the growth in absolute numbers in

1. The countries were Argentina, Brazil, Chile, Colombia, Ecuador, Guatemala and Peru (Barraclough and Domike, 1966, p. 407).

agriculture in most of the less-developed countries. In the five Central American countries, for example, the agricultural sector absorbed almost 45 per cent of the increase in the labour force during 1952 to 1964; services were second in labour absorption with almost 23 per cent; manufacturing was fourth with slightly over 11 per cent (Quiros, 1971, p. 126).

The unemployment problem is exacerbated by a population growth rate of 2·5 to 3 per cent or more, a rate prevailing in many of the less-developed countries over the past decade or two. Most of the industrialized countries (with the exception of the new-world regions during periods of major immigration) never experienced so rapid an increase in population. So long as the industrial sector cannot absorb productively these large increases in the labour force, the agricultural sector must provide increased opportunities for employment. This need will persist for many years into the future.

The imperative and the potential for employment creation through land reform

The transformation of a primarily agrarian population into one predominantly urban and industrial is usually a slow process – especially with high rates of population growth. For example, between 1937 and 1960, the percentage of the population employed in agriculture in Thailand declined by only 6 percentage points – from 84 to 78 per cent; comparable figures for India, 1931–61, are 70 to 65 per cent; for the Philippines, 1939–62, 75 to 66 per cent; for Japan, 1930–60, 41 to 26 per cent; for Mexico, 1940–60, 65 to 55 per cent; and for Indonesia, 1930–61, an increase from 68 to 73 per cent (Christensen, 1966, p. 122). Moreover, the farm population does not decline in absolute numbers until well after it has become a minority in the total population.[2]

Given the large proportion now dependent on agriculture and likely to be so dependent for decades into the future, and the relative capital-intensive developments in industry yielding insufficient new jobs, the creation of additional employment opportunities in the agricultural sector is certainly one of the goals of land reform. More specifically, land reform must lead

2. For an analysis of this phenomenon, see Dovring (1964).

to improved factor combinations and a better allocation of land and labour. Yet, the extent to which employment can be increased through redistributive land reforms depends very much on existing circumstances.

In the United Arab Republic, for instance, despite substantial reforms in the landholding pattern, major underemployment in the agricultural sector persists:

the supply of labour on the present land area is excessive in relation to labour requirements, although these are exceptionally high. Opinions differ as to the size of the true surplus (i.e. the number which could be removed from agriculture without reducing production). According to the First Five-Year Plan estimate, the surplus in 1960 amounted to 25 per cent of the male agricultural labour force, or 1·1 million out of a total of 4·4 million (Warriner, 1970, p. 607).

Although large amounts of land were distributed under the land reform in the United Arab Republic, land reform here as elsewhere could not create land that did not exist. Hence the employment problem remains acute.

A very different situation exists in most of Latin America. In most countries there, land distribution is so uneven that distributive reforms could have a major impact on employment creation in the agricultural sector. The misallocation of land and labour resources is striking – too few people and too much land in the large-farm subsector and too many people and too little land in the small-farm subsector.

In the five largely agrarian Central American countries (in about 1960), the small subfamily farms provided only 1·7 hectares of land per man whereas family farms had 13·4 hectares per man. The large, multifamily farms (producing crops mainly for export) contained 27·1 hectares per man when the labour of seasonal and migratory (often landless) workers is included, and 146 hectares per man when such labour is excluded (Quiros, 1971, p. 145). Under such circumstances it is not difficult to visualize the potential opportunities for increasing employment through a reallocation of land and people.

Without a land reform that will correct some of these basic misallocations, Central America's maldistribution of land continues and grows worse. During the region's intercensal period (1950–1960/64), 72 per cent of the increase in number of farms was in the subfamily class, but only 8 per cent of the increase of land in farms was in this category. At the other extreme, 9 per cent of the increase in farm numbers was in the large multifamily farm class, which accounted for 73 per cent of the new land in farms. Family sized farms accounted for 19 per cent of the total increment in both the number and in the area in farms (Quiros, 1971, p. 166).

Yet, land reform is not a one-shot, once-and-for-all cure for unemployment problems. Of all Latin American countries, Mexico had the first and the most massive land reform, re-distributing over the past fifty years more than 60 million hectares of land of which over 12 million hectares were crop-land (Dovring, 1970, pp. 19–20). Even here, most of the recent year additions to the rural labour force were absorbed by the small farm or the *ejido* subsectors. The annual growth rates for 1950 to 1960 in the number of people employed by the various size-of-farm sectors were as follows: private farms over 5 hectares, 0·4 per cent; private farms under 5 hectares, 4·3 per cent; *ejidos*, 2·0 per cent; all farms, 1·9 per cent (Barraclough and Schatan, 1970, p. 51; from Eckstein, 1969).

Without question, a great amount of involuntary leisure time is imposed on farmers in areas of dense population or in areas having a very uneven distribution of land. Even in Taiwan with its small-farm agriculture, the percentage of in-voluntary unemployment (estimated for 1961–2) ranges from zero on farms with 6·5 *chia*[3] (about 15·5 acres) or more, to 35 per cent on farms with less than one-half *chia* (about 1·2 acres). Employment calculations include both on-farm and off-farm work (Koo, 1968, p. 94). Koo also notes that there was no tendency for tenants to use some of their windfall gains in income, resulting from the land reform's reduction in rent payments, to reduce their labour inputs and increase their leisure time. This is further evidence that much of the existing under-employment or 'leisure' is indeed involuntary.

Of course, involuntary unemployment in Taiwan is relatively minor compared to that of some other areas. Algeria, for ex-

3. A *chia* is equal to 0·9699 hectare, or 2·3968 acres.

ample, has a labour force in the traditional sector of about 2·1 million persons. It is estimated that 75 per cent of the available labour time is unutilized (Foster, 1970, p. 15, from Griffin, 1965, p. 242). Data from Venezuela show that in the mid-1960s, persons working in agriculture were employed for only about 50 per cent of their assumed 300 man-days of available work time (Wing, 1970, p. 45). A 1955 study in the Philippines concludes that

operators and family members together supplied the equivalent of 28·3 man-months of potential labor force of which only 8·9 months were utilized in productive farm labor, 6·2 months for off-farm employment opportunities, and 13·2 months remained idle (Koone and Gleeck, 1970, p. 22).

And so it is in country after country.[4] Sufficient employment opportunities are not being generated for the growing number of people in rural areas. Also, industrialization, especially with its capital-intensive tendencies[5] will simply not create enough new jobs for the growing numbers moving to the cities. From the mid-1950s to the mid-1960s the rate of output in manufacturing in the less-industrialized countries has grown from one-and-a-half to two times as fast as the rate of growth in employment (United Nations, 1970, p. 278). Although the employment–output ratio in manufacturing was higher in the less-industrialized than in the industrial countries, and was somewhat higher in Asia than in Latin America, it was insufficient to absorb the large increases in the urban labour force. In some countries relatively high rates of growth in output were actually accompanied by a decrease in employment. Experience of the past few decades indicates that in the developing countries an automatic mechanism linking increases in production to equivalent increases in employment does not exist. The fact of the matter is that modern industrialization not only creates employment but also eliminates many

4. For an analysis of these problems (and the necessity for generating more employment) in African agriculture, see Eicher *et al.* (1970).

5. Although undoubtedly an extreme case, in Iraq agriculture and petroleum each contributed about 25 per cent to Gross National Product in 1956. Agriculture accounted for over 80 per cent of the active labour force, while 1 per cent or less was employed by the petroleum industry (Treakle, 1970, p. 5).

jobs as handicraft industries are replaced by assembly lines (Myrdal, 1965).

The prospect that unemployment and under-employment will become increasingly serious during the next two or three decades (as a result of the combination of a rapidly growing labor force and a pervasive bias toward a capital-intensive pattern of investment) is one of the critical problems that needs to be illuminated by better understanding of agriculture–industry interactions under the unique conditions confronting the contemporary developing countries (Johnston, 1970, p. 386).

A few theoretical examples will demonstrate how difficult it is for nations confronting a 3 per cent population growth rate and having 50 per cent or more of their population in agriculture to absorb the total natural increase in non-farm employment. If a country's population is now 50 per cent rural and 50 per cent urban, then given a 3 per cent annual population growth, the urban population would have to grow by 6 per cent annually in order to hold constant the absolute numbers now in the rural sector. With a 75 per cent to 25 per cent rural–urban split, the urban population would have to grow by 12 per cent annually in order for the rural population to remain constant.

There is simply insufficient capital to create urban facilities and jobs at a 12 per cent or even perhaps at a 6 per cent rate. *Thus the agricultural sector in the less-developed countries must continue to provide increased employment opportunities for many years to come.* Absolute numbers of rural people decline only in later stages of development, and only then is it necessary to reorganize agricultural production to decrease its labour requirements.

However, major efforts are required in order to create employment opportunities in non-farm sectors as rapidly as possible. There is a definite limit, already being approached in some countries, to the employment creation possibilities in agriculture. The resolution of the unemployment problem rests ultimately with a dynamic urban sector rather than with changes that can be introduced in the agricultural sector. Such basic reorientations in the industrial sector, however, may themselves be impossible without a restructuring of the employment and income-earning opportunities in agriculture and the demand consequences inherent in such changes.

Obstacles to labour absorption on large estates

As pointed out previously, under conditions prevailing in many of the less-developed countries, the early phases of agricultural development should rely on labour-intensive techniques and yield increasing technical innovations which increase agricultural production without displacing labour prematurely from agriculture. Yield-increasing inputs, efficient service institutions for agricultural production and marketing, and the minimization of labour-replacing mechanization are requisites for such a policy.

Under existing conditions, however, and especially in large estate systems characteristic of much of Latin America, it has been difficult to gain acceptance of such policies. Labour-saving machine technology is available from the industrialized countries. So long as investment decisions are made on the basis of private profit, large-farm entrepreneurs may find it in their best economic interest to import labour-saving machinery. In fact it may be easier to transplant this type of technology than the biological type, which often requires additional research before it can be adapted to the specific ecological conditions in new areas. The wide range of available production techniques now affecting employment contrasts with the more restricted options open to agricultural entrepreneurs in the nineteenth century. In the earlier period, labour-saving technology was largely a response to a scarcity of labour, and the major innovations emerged within the industrializing regions of the time – especially England, the United States and Western Europe.

However, machines alone are not responsible for all the labour displacement. Other inputs can also displace labour. 'Chemical weeding in coffee plantations reduced the permanent labour force by 50 to 60 per cent and resulted in an increase in the use of seasonal labour during the harvest season' (Quiros, 1971, p. 214). Because of this and other innovations, Guatemalan coffee production increased by 157 per cent between 1950 and 1964, with an increase in area cultivated of 85·1 per cent, but an increase in total employment of only 6·6 per cent (Quiros, 1971, p. 220).

In addition to the sequential nature of peak labor requirements in export crops, two additional factors account for the recent growth in migratory labor pools. One is that the export sector itself grew by almost 700,000 hectares in 1966–68 relative to 1950. A second reason is that . . . the capital-intensive technology currently in use in large-scale enterprises intensifies the need for temporary and seasonal labor, although it reduces the permanent labor requirements (Quiros, 1971, p. 243a).

If agriculture were strictly comparable to industry, the employment dilemma outlined in the preceding pages would seem all but insoluble. In certain branches of modern industry, capital-intensive developments are frequently inevitable because the necessary machine technology is that used in and available from the industrialized countries. This technology may limit the substitution of factors, e.g. labour for capital, in production processes as well as offer considerable economies of scale for the larger enterprises.

If agricultural production were similarly restricted, there would be few alternatives to capital-intensive developments in this sector since agriculture in the industrial countries is also capital intensive. But agriculture is different. Alternative means of economic organization in agriculture permit greater flexibility in production processes. Factor proportions (land, labour and capital) can more nearly be utilized in a manner consistent with their relative cost and availability. Market imperfections continue to obstruct more rational use of factors, but it is precisely at these imperfections (in land, labour and capital markets) that land reform is directed.

The assumption that only a few alternative processes and a limited range of factor substitutions are possible does not seem to fit the characteristics of agriculture (Eckaus, 1955). A major problem is that the large, often redundant, agricultural labour force in many of the less-developed countries lacks the economic and political power to gain control (either ownership or rental) over sufficient land and capital resources to increase its productivity. Present distribution patterns in many of these countries show gross misallocations in terms of resource availabilities. In Latin American countries, for example, 30 to 40 per cent of the active agricultural population typically lives on and works less than 10 per cent of the land.

Why don't managers of plantations and large estates and farmers with large extensions of land employ more labour? There are many possible reasons. Farm owners may have outside interests that hold greater economic importance for them than farming. Abundant labour is not always cheap labour; minimum wages and a variety of social welfare laws may increase the price of labour.

When the Morgan Report on wages was accepted by the Nigerian government in 1964, government wages were increased 20 per cent and private estates and plantations increased their wage rates and *quietly* reduced their labor force. One private estate in Nigeria, for example, responded to higher wages by laying off 400 workers and substituting chemical spraying of weeds for the machete technique (Eicher *et al.*, 1970, p. 28).

A large, unskilled hired labour force becomes difficult to manage on labour-intensive enterprises. It also increases the risk in dealing with expensive machinery, improved livestock, and modern production practices which require constant use of judgement on the part of labourers. In these circumstances, owners of large farms will frequently reduce their labour force and move toward capital-intensive, mechanized operations with a relatively small force of skilled workers, supplemented when needed by seasonal labour (Schmid, 1967).

Apparently on the assumption that a developed agriculture is a mechanized one and that developing countries should have the same factor proportions now existing in the agriculture of developed countries, government policy often encourages importation of farm machinery through favourable foreign exchange rates. Furthermore, most of the credit for machinery purchase as well as for other purposes goes to the commercial farm sector (more creditworthy by bankers' standards), with inflation often making effective interest rates minimal or even negative. In other words, monetary, fiscal and exchange rate policies often discourage the utilization of the abundant labour resources; these policies frequently intensify the unemployment problems by encouraging imports of capital-intensive machine technology. Resource misallocations and poor performance are not surprising given the underlying assumptions and the monopolized control over land and capital. But the profitable course for the individual entrepreneur results in costs to society which cannot forever be postponed (Dorner and Kanel, 1971).

From the point of view of the nation or the society as a whole, elevating the basic quality and capacity of the human resource must be a primary concern. This can be accomplished only if the under-privileged masses are provided with opportunities for productive employment. The quality of the people 'produced' in the process must be a central criterion of economic development. The generation of economic growth without the institutional changes represented by land reform has in most cases been unable to meet this criterion.

Agricultural development, envisaged only fifteen years ago as a process of socio-economic advance, has been narrowed to the scope of increased agricultural output, while man, in feudal times a tool for the exploitation of the land and thus an essential appendage to the land, seems gradually to be losing his relevance to agriculture; and this, despite the fact that in the underdeveloped countries there is no alternative place for him in urban industries and services (Jacoby, 1971, p. 13).

Labour absorption capabilities of a small-farm agriculture

In a system built on private property in land, the size of farm operating units is a basic determinant in the development of a labour-intensive agriculture. Data from the late 1950s for India (Madhya Pradesh), the US (Illinois), and Chile (Central Valley) show the following relationships: farms in the smallest size-class had 1·6, 74, and 1·1 acres per worker while those in the largest size class had 15·6, 219, and 16·6 acres per worker, for the three countries respectively (Kanel, 1967, p. 29).[6] These data certainly indicate some adaptation to the different factor proportions existing in these countries. They also, however, illustrate the greater employment capacity of small-farm units,

6. These studies were conducted in areas of relatively uniform conditions of soil or, in the case of Chile, total acres were converted to 'equivalent irrigated acres'.

even though output *per man* may be (and usually is) lower on the small units. These figures also suggest a wider range of production techniques in the agriculture of the less-developed countries: for example, the ratio of acres per man on large over small farms is about 3 in the United States but is about 10 and 15 in the cases of India and Chile, respectively.

This greater labour absorption on small units is also reported for Taiwan. Although the farms in Taiwan's larger size categories are relatively small, the average amount of labour input per crop hectare is consistently larger on small holdings. Farms of less than 0·5 hectares averaged 387 units of labour per crop hectare. As farm size increased, the average use of labour per crop hectare consistently declined. The largest size group, 2·0 hectares and over, averaged only 146 units of labour per crop hectare (Koo, 1970, p. 46).

A study of the Chateaulin area of Brittany reports that

when one moved from holdings of less than 5 hectares to those of more than 25, the number of workers per 100 hectares fell from 105 to 18·7, the number of per annum working hours per hectare from 1500 to 480. Working capital also fell, but less markedly, from 210,000 to 119,000 francs, and gross yield from Index 163 to 88 (average for the area: 100) (Cépède, 1971, p. 245, citing a study by J. B. Chombart de Lauwe and F. Morvan, 1954).

The man–land ratio on the ex-*haciendas* of the Bolivian side of Lake Titicaca is more than eight times the ratio on the other side of the lake in Peru (Burke, 1970). Although the Bolivian *haciendas* were apparently more densely populated than those in Peru even before the Bolivian reform of 1953, the population on the Bolivian side seems to have further increased by more than 50 per cent during the period 1953–65. Meanwhile, the area on the Peruvian side was declared an agrarian reform zone in 1965 with the stipulation that large landowners could retain more land if they paid *campesinos* legal minimum wages. This provision resulted in *campesino* firings and evictions. Despite the much greater population density, the Bolivian peasants produced only 20 per cent less marketable surplus per hectare as their counterparts produced on the more extensive farmed estates in Peru, and their level of living was higher than that of the nearby Peruvian peasants.

Commenting on Mexico, Dovring notes that small-scale, labour-intensive production is less costly than large-scale production in terms of the goods that are scarce in the Mexican economy. The large private farms are using more of the hardware that might otherwise have been invested toward even more rapid industrialization of the country. 'There is no doubt,' concludes Dovring, 'that the owners or holders of large private farms make a good income by using more machines and somewhat less labour, but they render a less useful service to the struggling and developing economy of a low-income, capital-scarce country' (Dovring, 1970, pp. 50–51).

For West Pakistan, Johnston and Cownie make a strong case for employment of more labour rather than more tractors in agriculture. They argue that 'the existence of yield-increasing innovations (e.g. the new varieties and fertilizers) which are neutral to scale and consistent with the existing systems of small-scale agriculture increases the advantages of the labour-intensive capital-saving alternative' (Johnston and Cownie, 1969, p. 573).

Additional cases could be cited, but it is quite clear that under a system of private property in land, a small-farm agriculture can absorb more labour than a large-farm agriculture. Some have cautioned that a small farm agriculture of peasant proprietors may lead to an excess of capital equipment on small holdings, i.e. much duplication and under-utilization of buildings and equipment. However, the Japanese case shows that mechanization can be adapted to fit small farms if research is specifically directed to that end. Or, on the other hand, a reorganization of a large-farm system on co-operative or communitarian principles may be able to assure both labour absorption and efficiency in the use of capital equipment.

Agricultural production processes, as mentioned, have characteristics which invalidate many comparisons with developments in industry. The superiority of a large-farm system, argued on the basis of economies of scale, is an old idea.

Marshall and Mill expressed serious doubts about its validity, but as Owen has pointed out, 'It is probably fair to say that most economists have since attempted to resolve his [Marshall's] dilemma by avoiding it' (Owen, 1966, p. 48).

With regard to the nature of employment in agriculture, Owen quotes John Stuart Mill:

Agriculture . . . is not susceptible of so great a division of occupations as many branches of manufactures, because its different operations cannot possibly be simultaneous. One man cannot be always ploughing, another sowing, and another reaping. A workman who only practised one agricultural operation would be idle eleven months of the year. The same person may perform them all in succession, and have, in most climates, a considerable amount of unoccupied time (Owen, 1966, p. 49).[7]

Labour absorption in different systems of agricultural organization

There seems little question that the most labour-absorptive system of economic organization in agriculture is a small-farm (operating unit) system. This may be a sharecropping system such as prevailed in Japan and Taiwan before the reforms of the 1950s[8]. This type of land tenure arrangement is still very common in much of Southeast Asia and in many other parts of the world. Or it may be a system of small, privately owned farms as in Japan and Taiwan after the reforms.[9]

There may, however, be a major difference in the labour-absorptive potential of a conventional sharecropping system and one based on peasant proprietorship or other secure form of tenure. The greater tenure security and the incentives to

7. Mill's insight has been elaborated by Brewster (1950).

8. Although sharecropping systems can absorb a great deal of labour, they have many undesirable features and are not recommended as a base upon which to develop the agricultural economy.

9. Although the basic trend over the past several decades has been toward farm enlargement, this was not the case in the United States until after 1940, and even later in most of Europe and in Japan. Japan's total agricultural population declined by 4·5 per cent annually while crop area per farm person increased by 3·7 per cent annually (compound rates for the period 1950–65) (Schaub, 1970, p. 18; see also Voelkner, 1970).

which it gives rise may lead to the intensification of cultivation practices. Under appropriate climatic conditions, multiple cropping may become more widespread. This can greatly increase the demand for labour (indeed it may at times lead to seasonal labour shortages).

In Chekiang Province in China in the mid-1950s, the change from single to double cropping of rice increased the demand for labor by 80 per cent. The labor requirements for triple cropping were up to two to three times greater than for double cropping in Taiwan, depending on which of several rotations are involved (Dalrymple, 1971, p. 44, citing Walker, 1965, p. 64 and Cheng, 1970, p. 10).

A system of communally owned land where parcels are allocated to individual families for their private use and cultivation may also be highly labour-intensive. This is characteristic of the Mexican *ejidos*, many Indian communities in other Latin American countries, as well as most tribal systems in tropical Africa. In contrast to these small operating-unit systems, the large private estate operated as a unit is the least labour-absorptive. This appears to be the case even when it is operated along traditional lines, and it is definitely the case under conditions of modernization and active entrepreneurship.

Despite all its imperfections, peasant proprietorship provides considerably more security to the agricultural population than ownership vested in large landowners. An agriculture of landowning peasants provides a shelter for the masses of people for whom outside employment is not available. It absorbs population increases up to the limits of capacity to support life. On the other hand, it does not necessarily act as a barrier to out-migration when employment opportunities appear elsewhere. . . . It permits the use of new technological opportunities in farming, . . . but those who have no alternatives or who cannot or are not ready to utilize new technology have access to subsistence. By contrast, in an agriculture dominated by large landowners, continued peasant employment depends on employer decisions, and for a variety of reasons, more active management by these landowners often leads to a relatively labor-saving path of modernization. These considerations are very important in the earlier stages of development when the growth in non-agricultural employment opportunities is low and the bulk of the population depends on agriculture (Kanel, 1971).

In those countries where part or most of the agricultural

land has been 'socialized', the situation with respect to labour absorption is quite mixed. It depends on population density (and on its regional distribution), on the decisions of government officials, and on the specificity of legislation dealing with these questions. In general, the various cooperative-collective and/or state farming systems occupy a position between the two extremes of labour absorption described above.

The possibilities for affecting labour absorption in the agricultural sector of socialized economies are illustrated in the economic organization of agriculture in Yugoslavia, Rumania and Poland. All three countries implemented comprehensive land reforms during the decade following the Second World War. In Yugoslavia, most of the land remains in private ownership: about 86 per cent of the cultivated land is in privately owned peasant farms (a ten-hectare ceiling was imposed in 1953) while the remainder is incorporated in worker-managed enterprises called social estates. In 1969, there were slightly more than 2000 social estates and over 2·5 million private, individual holdings. The social estates held 14 per cent of the cultivated land, had 72 per cent of all the tractors in use on Yugoslavia's farms, and employed 3 per cent of the agricultural labour force. The family holdings held 86 per cent of the cultivated land, had 28 per cent of the tractors, and employed 97 per cent of the agricultural labour force (Federal Institute for Statistics, 1970, p. 44). This dualistic policy is deliberate. The tax structure encourages mechanization and labour efficiency on the social estates, and promotes production intensification (sometimes for different commodities than those most commonly found on the social estates), increased employment, and labour absorption on the small family farms.

In 1969 Rumania had slightly over 20 per cent of its *arable* land in state farms, 75 per cent[10] in agricultural producer cooperatives (collectives), and less than 5 per cent in privately held individual farms. The latter, however, held over 9 per cent of the *total* agricultural area, having a relatively larger proportion in meadows and pastures. These private farms, located

10. A little more than 8 per cent of the total arable land (11 per cent of all arable land controlled by the collectives) is given over for personal use to members of agricultural producer cooperatives.

mainly in the hilly and mountainous regions of the country, employed approximately 10 per cent of the agricultural labour force.

Rumania also maintains a deliberate dual policy in its two major subsectors of agriculture. The state farms have slightly over six hectares of arable land per worker. By contrast, the agricultural producer cooperatives have less than 1·5 hectares of arable land per worker. In other words, the man–land ratio is over four times greater on the collectives (Central Statistical Board, 1970, pp. 146–7).

In Poland, individual family farms predominate. This small-farm sector includes 85 per cent of the arable land, employs 92 per cent of the economically active agricultural population, and produces 88 per cent of the gross agricultural output. State farms have slightly over 13 per cent of the land (the remaining land is operated by the relatively small sector of producer cooperatives), employ about 4 per cent of the agricultural work force, and produce 11 per cent of the total output. The man–land ratio on the small farms is about four times greater than on the state farms (Lipski, 1969, pp. 32–8). The state farms in Rumania and Poland and the social estates in Yugoslavia are much less labour absorptive than the agriculture producer cooperatives or the individual peasant farms. But this is by deliberate design of public policy.[11]

A dual policy with respect to employment in the agricultural sector is neither a socialist principle nor one confined in practice to socialist countries. Even after a widespread land reform, Mexico has followed a dual policy toward the agricultural sector, with much more of the capital and credit (but much less of the manpower) utilized by the larger private farms than by the small private farms or the *ejidos* (Dovring, 1970). In con-

11. Labour utilization in agriculture should be evaluated in a context wider than that pertaining only to work on the farm. The broader issue concerns the mobilization of labour and capital for the development of rural industry and of social overhead capital (or infrastructure) in rural areas. Although evidence is not readily available, it would seem that either a relatively egalitarian system of family farms or a socialized system has the advantage over a large-estate system. For an interesting discussion of this point comparing the US South with both the US North and Latin America, see Thiesenhusen (1969).

trast, Japan and Taiwan, starting of course from a very different base and tenure structure, were much more successful in implementing a relatively uniform policy based on small units and a labour-intensive agriculture. These last two countries, through intensive land use practices, including double and triple cropping, were able to employ their growing populations in the agricultural sector until the industrial sector was large enough to absorb more of the rural labour force.

The pre-reform agricultural situations reflect a policy of dualism in most countries. Often a large-farm, commercial, capital-intensive sector produces for export while a small-farm, labour-intensive sector produces for the internal market. Sometimes, however, this dualism exists within the sector producing primarily for the internal market. In either event, this pre-reform dualism has not functioned well in providing sufficient employment opportunities, given population growth rates and the relatively slow growth of employment opportunities in industry.

Post-reform dualism may be more viable. The critical variables associated with the possible success or failure of such a dualistic, post-reform structure are the size and the rate of growth of the industrial sector, the proportion of the population in agriculture, and the growth rate of the total population. In the East European countries discussed, all these variables appear favourable: substantial industrial sectors, slightly under 50 per cent of the population in agriculture, and a relatively slow (1·0 to 1·5 per cent annual) population growth rate. The conditions in Mexico are much less favourable despite a rapidly expanding industrial sector. The major difference is the much more rapid rate of population growth – averaging over 3 per cent annually over the 1950–68 period (Schaub, 1970, p. 11).

One of the objectives of land reform must be the increased agricultural employment opportunities that can be created within a reorganized tenure structure. The specific form of such a reorganization is an issue to be decided by the people in each country. In actual practice, people must deal with the agricultural system as it is and as might reasonably be modified, not as it could be if there was a 'clean slate' from which to begin.

This is true whether the present tenure structure is altered by revolutionary or more orderly means. The rural people with their specific skills or lack of them, the physical resources with peculiar capacities, obstacles and locations, the attitudes and beliefs generated by unique historical antecedents – all these comprise the real world situation and they cannot be wished away. Present man–land ratios, existing land tenure arrangements, distributions of income and wealth, distribution of population throughout a country's agricultural regions, size and potential of the industrial base, the proportion of the total population dependent on agriculture, and population growth rates are some of the variables determining the potential employment benefits from land reform as well as the tenure reorganization attainable

5 Land Reform, Investments and Productivity

The relationships between land reform, increased investments and productivity are not always direct and positive, especially in the short run. Some countries without any land reforms have registered sharp increases in agricultural output, while others with major reforms have lagged behind. As noted earlier, land reform is neither a variable easily manipulable by governments nor a measure introduced with the single objective of increasing output from the agricultural sector.

Agricultural output: pre-reform and post-reform

Of the fifty-four countries included in a US Department of Agriculture study, six had annual growth rates in total volume of agricultural production in the period 1950–68 of 5 per cent or more. These were five countries in Latin America and Israel (with a fantastic growth rate of 9·3 per cent). Of the five Latin American nations, one has carried out a comprehensive land reform (Mexico), another has implemented a more modest but still substantial reform programme (Venezuela), and the other three have done very little in the field of basic structural reforms (Guatemala, Nicaragua and Ecuador) (USDA, 1970, p. 11).

By way of contrast, Cuba carried out basic structural reforms in the early 1960s and experienced sharp declines in agricultural production, at least in the first several years following the reform. There are few reliable data for later years, but the per capita agricultural production index in the years immediately following the reform did drop sharply. From a base of 100 (1952–3 and 1954–5) this index rose to 133 in 1960–61, then dropped to 86, 69 and 63 in the years 1961–2, 1962–3 and 1963–4, respectively (Gayoso, 1970, p. 74, quoting from US Department of Agriculture, 1963b, p. 11). The extent to which this performance record of Cuban agriculture was influenced by negative US policies toward the Cuban revolution cannot be determined. But this influence should not be discounted in evaluating the Cuban experience.

Such a setback is hardly unique, however, and is usually temporary. After the 1958 revolution in Iraq, crop production declined and remained low for a number of years (Treakle, 1970, p. 57). In Mexico, following major land distributions in the 1930s, the private sector was evidently depressed in 1940 (a census year). Dovring (1969) reports that

ongoing land reform in the thirties, and the consequent uncertainty of many landowners about how much land they could count on to retain must have acted as a deterrent against normal production. With the reduction in the land reform activity in the 1940s, the large farms were able to recover relatively rapidly from their depressed state, hence the high increase in output rate in the 1940s (p. 13).

After the Bolivian revolution of 1952, measured and reported agricultural output was also lower. In recent years performance has been much improved, and even in the 1950s the likely explanations for the apparent drop in agricultural output are a possible reduction in marketings (the peasants consumed more) and several years of severe drought (Clark, 1970, pp. 52–62). Of course, some of Bolivia's farm lands were actually idled and some under-utilized because of the turmoil created by the peasant takeover in the countryside. However, peasants worked the remaining lands more intensively than before. Even farm produce marketed may not have fallen as much as indicated by market estimates since there was a lag in statistical reporting of produce flowing through the new post-reform marketing channels.

Apparent or real declines in post-reform production are usually temporary and are not surprising. Reform, especially when associated with major political and social revolutionary upheavals, can be a disruptive process. Also, many other services are needed once land is redistributed – the old service structures, geared to pre-reform production and tenure conditions, will not fit the needs of the new, reformed system.

These four countries (Cuba, Iraq, Mexico and Bolivia), all

characterized by a feudal-like system before the reform and all abruptly changed by revolution, stand in contrast to countries characterized by sharecropper systems of cultivation, with services geared to a small farm agriculture. As Christensen (1968) reports:

Land reform in Taiwan was successful in increasing agricultural output and productivity for several reasons. Perhaps most important is the fact that supporting services to provide extension education, marketing, credit, and production requisites had been built up. In addition, tenant farmers who became landowners were experienced farm operators accustomed to making managerial decisions (p. 89).

The existence of this supportive service structure reflects the history of Japanese colonial policies designed to expand output (see Hayami and Ruttan, 1970). Pre-reform Taiwan also had a working cadastral system which greatly facilitated implementation of the reform. Various grades and categories of land were identified, individual boundaries were recorded, and land rights were registered. Since the cadastral record was based on surveys carried out long before the land reform, there were no questions about its objectivity. The cadastral system and its measures were accepted by both landlords and tenants, making it 'possible for the government to step in to establish a standard yield for every grade of paddy field' (Koo, 1968, p. 32). Yield standards of course facilitated the setting of land payment rates and land rental rates as required by the reform law. As a result of these favourable conditions, instead of a slump in output following the reform, output increased at an accelerated rate.

The Japanese record is equally impressive. Here too farmers received new incentives to intensify productive efforts as they became owners of land rather than tenants or sharecroppers. Although suffering from the exhaustion and destruction of the Second World War, Japan nevertheless enjoyed many of the same favourable circumstances existing in Taiwan, and here too the rate of agricultural output following the reform accelerated (Voelkner, 1970).

Although climatic, cultural and tenure conditions were quite different, the United Arab Republic presents yet another case where increases in output followed land reform rather directly and immediately. Cotton acreage and output fell initially, but these losses were soon recovered and the rate of output accelerated even though acreage devoted to cotton remained lower. Significantly, the output index of foodstuffs – especially fruits and vegetables – rose faster than that of total agricultural output. This differential growth points up another important consequence of land reform: reform in tenure structures usually results in a change in cropping patterns, reflecting peasant purposes, new incentives, and improved peasant incomes. Frequently, the output of export crops falls while that of food crops increases. There may be, as the case of the United Arab Republic exemplifies, a new emphasis on crops of higher nutritional value (Raup, 1967, p. 285).

These cases offer a few illustrations of agricultural production levels following land tenure reforms. The extent to which reform alone can be credited with or blamed for these production consequences is difficult to measure. Many other complex and interrelated factors influence the levels and shifts in farm output.

Farm prices and production response

In evaluating output increases or decreases accompanying land reform, the influence of farm price levels on investments and output cannot be disputed. The level of product prices influences the amount produced. Farmers may shift from one crop to another, or may decrease the use of inputs given lower farm product prices (or anticipated lower prices).

Land tenure arrangements influence farmer response to changing prices. An FAO (1963) study concludes that

price response was usually greater among owner-operators than among tenants. Tenants paying a fixed rent were likely to benefit more from price incentives and therefore to show a greater response to price changes than sharecroppers. . . . Producer price policies were therefore generally more successful where they had been preceded by land reform measures (p. 2).

Therefore, perhaps more important than prices *per se*, under most circumstances of agricultural development in the world today, is the incentive structure provided by the tenure system. Raup (1967) has stated these requirements as follows:

How can tenure security contribute to capital formation? By making the use of a productive asset the preclusive right of an individual or a group. This security of expectation is crucial for biological forms of capital, for slow-maturing enterprises, and for undertakings involving numerous incremental additions made successively over many production cycles. . . . The major impact of land tenure arrangements is upon decisions regarding the allocation of labor time. The cultivator can invest his labor in the farm firm, or in the household. He can invest resulting income in productive assets, or in consumption. He can do this within a short time-horizon, or he can take the long view (pp. 273–4).

Unfortunately, very few specific studies of less-developed countries have inquired into the relationship between land tenure security and levels of farm investment and production. Research in two rural areas of Costa Rica does show a positive relationship between increasing levels of tenure security (measured along a scale with nine different levels ranging from illegal squatting to a legally recognized and registered land title) and improved farm performance (measured in terms of investment and gross output). Field studies in the two areas, one settled in the early 1900s and the other settled between 1940 and 1960, show that increasing levels of tenure security, especially a legally recognized and registered title to the land, account for most of the difference in performance levels. Among the various factors which are positively correlated with increased agricultural output, full title to the land is the single most important one (Salas, *et al.*, 1970, pp. 22–3; see also Thome, 1971b).

The Costa Rican studies were conducted in newly settled areas producing subsistence crops and livestock. Tenure rights under these conditions may be less secure and less certain than under an old established sharecropping system such as existed in the pre-reform rice culture in Taiwan. Even under share-cropping, from 1920 to 1930, agricultural output in Taiwan grew at a rate of almost 4 per cent annually (Christensen, 1968, pp. 2–3). Concurrently, however, prices were relatively stable and at low levels. The important factors explaining this good production performance were the basic infrastructural works that existed, the scientific practices being introduced, and the markets available. Japan took all the rice and sugar that could be produced (Hayami and Ruttan, 1970).

In the United States, gross investments in agriculture (for improvements to land and buildings, implements and machinery, harness and saddlery, and livestock inventory changes) increased from $51 million (in 1910–14 dollars) in 1800 to $190 million in 1850 and to $631 million by 1900 (USDA, 1963a). It is of great significance for development to recognize that much of this capital was produced through the direct efforts of farmers themselves – converting their own labour into capital structures. It is also of interest that fluctuation in farm prices and attendant changing prospects for farming profits did not greatly influence this capital growth process (Dorner, 1971c, p. 410). Tostlebe (1957) shows that 'between 1870 and 1900 prices paid to farmers were declining much of the time, yet during those years real capital formation proceeded at a faster pace than at any subsequent time.'[1]

Another consideration relevant to this discussion of prices is that owners of large tracts of land may have full knowledge of non-agricultural investment opportunities in the economy and may have the ability and the interest to shift investment funds to those places where returns are highest. This response would be expected under competitive market conditions; economists consider such behaviour rational and desirable, *assuming* that all prices in the economy are indeed competitively determined. On the other hand, a farmer of a small family unit may have neither knowledge nor opportunity for investing anywhere except in his farming operation. Alternative investment possibilities are not as likely to attract investment funds from a family-farm system of agriculture, and agricultural production will be less sensitive to price level changes (although it will remain sensitive to relative prices among agricultural commodities and acreage shifts may take place). A surplus for investments in other sectors can be obtained from a small, family-farm agriculture through other means than direct in-

1. This corresponds to the era of homesteading under the homestead law of 1862. The prospects for obtaining landownership undoubtedly provided major incentives to many farmers and prospective farmers throughout this period.

vestments by individuals. This topic is fully discussed later in this chapter, but it is well to point out here that such other means will either give the state control over such an investible surplus, or will allow the surplus to accrue to entrepreneurs in the industrial sector (as a result of terms of trade unfavourable to farm produce).

Frequently, a lag or an acceleration in agricultural output is attributed primarily to changes in price levels. Prices can be an important factor, but they are only one of many. Tenure security, availability of new yield-increasing inputs, access to markets, farmers' know-how and awareness of opportunities – these are other important elements. Above all, tenure security is an important element in creating incentives for increased investments and production.

Land tenure influences in the export and subsistence sectors

Some countries achieving the most rapid increases in agricultural output have done little to alter their land tenure structures. Increased output, however, may come primarily from the export sector, as was indeed the case in the three countries – Guatemala, Nicaragua and Ecuador – mentioned earlier in this chapter.

Many of the developing countries have a dual structure in agriculture, and rapid rates of increase in the modern sector may fail to produce the spread effects benefiting the entire economy because the forward and backward linkages do not exist. This is especially true in cases where the modern, commercial, large farm-plantation sector produces primarily for export while the small-farm sector produces for subsistence and for the domestic market. An analysis of this phenomenon is available for the five countries in the Central American Common Market – Costa Rica, Nicaragua, El Salvador, Honduras and Guatemala. In these countries in the mid-1960s, the small subfamily and family farms produced 75 per cent of the basic grains (domestic subsistence crops), whereas the medium and large multifamily farms produced over 77 per cent of several of the major export crops (coffee, cotton and sugar cane) (Quiros, 1971, p. 150).

Data and statistical time series are not available for a

detailed documentation of the way in which the Central American export sector competes for resources with the domestic sector. However, Quiros presents several case studies of the phenomenon. In one area of Costa Rica, in the years 1959–69, land area devoted to banana production increased approximately twelve times while corn marketed decreased from over 5000 tons to less than 1000 tons annually (Quiros, 1971, p. 179). During the cotton boom in Nicaragua from 1952–67, cotton acreage expanded rapidly while a nearly equivalent drop in acreage planted to basic grains occurred (the coefficient of determination, R^2, was 0·998) (Quiros, 1971, pp. 186–7).

These case studies, says Quiros (1971),

represent a modern manifestation of the manner in which the export sector has always expanded at the expense of the weaker traditional sector. . . . The addition or expansion of an export crop has seldom resulted in a permanent opportunity for the traditional sector to enhance its development alternatives (p. 189).

Most efforts for improving agriculture in such dual systems are devoted to export crops, as reflected in the differential yield increases. For the five Central American countries from 1950–67, the average annual percentage growth in yields per hectare of the major export crops was 2·8 while that of the major domestic crops was 0·1. During the same period, total output of the major export crops grew by 4·7 per cent annually while that of domestic crops averaged only a 2·9 per cent yearly increase (Quiros, 1971, pp. 205–7).

Recently, and in part as a response to the enlarged market resulting from the Common Market policies, the large farm-plantation sector has also moved into production of some subsistence crops, especially rice and corn. As this happens, subsistence opportunities in agriculture are displaced in a manner similar to the displacement which occurs with the expansion of export crops.

Governments, in trying to resolve balance-of-payments problems, sometimes grant concessions to foreign companies for the purpose of increasing the production and marketing of agricultural exports. In 1966 the government of the Dominican

Republic was negotiating with a consortium of United States companies a long-term rental contract for operating a large area of excess sugar cane land. The companies insisted upon a contract guarantee that they not be pressured to hire undue amounts of labour and that they be allowed to operate 'efficiently' with modern mechanization. The Dominican economy is largely agricultural, and estimates of unemployment in the country at the time exceeded 30 per cent. While such a contract arrangement might help solve a short-run balance-of-payments problem, it would do little to create opportunities for the unemployed (Dorner, 1971a, p. 21).

There are, of course, many positive factors for development inherent in a rapid expansion of agricultural exports. However, there are also possible disadvantages to be evaluated. Johnston (1970) discusses Bairoch's (1964) concern with the bias toward reliance on agricultural exports:

The reduction in costs of transport has also contributed to what Bairoch regards as an 'excessive' development of agricultural exports which has tended to have adverse effect on the diffusion process, especially when export production was concentrated in foreign-owned plantations: (a) profits were often exported instead of being reinvested in the expansion of local industries, (b) expatriate firms depended upon foreign sources of supply for agricultural equipment, (c) there was a minimum favorable impact on local subsistence agriculture because plantation techniques were often not susceptible to being generalized within the local agricultural economy, and frequently increased demand for food was met by imports, and (d) there was weak incentive for creation of local industries for processing agricultural raw materials or minerals (p. 389).

Under conditions of duality in farm size and tenure structures, agricultural policies frequently favour the large producing units. The inequalities in economic power (combined with rapid population growth and relative capital-intensive developments in industry) leave the mass of the population excluded from the accruing benefits. Only through land reforms and government intervention can the distribution of benefits be improved, and in the longer run only a more equal distribution can keep the development process moving forward.

Investment and productivity on small farms

The previous two chapters outlined certain advantages of a small-farm system in providing more employment, a more equitable distribution of income (at least in early stages of development), and a more relevant demand structure for the growing manufacturing sector. Yet all these advantages may seem inconsequential if a small-farm system cannot generate sufficient investments and the necessary increases in agricultural output both for export and for feeding rapidly growing populations.

Small family-farm units exist in most countries irrespective of the tenure form dominating a country's agricultural system. The discussions that follow deal primarily with cases retaining private property in land, generally under an individual farm operator system. Productivity comparisons are made of small and large farms both before and after reforms.

Many agricultural technicians and economists believe that large farms are more 'efficient', and indeed they are in terms of certain measures of productivity and efficiency. It is true that labour productivity is consistently higher on larger farms, but this measure is hardly relevant to policy in a labour-surplus economy. Higher labour productivity on large farms results primarily from mechanization and labour-saving techniques. Land-saving technologies – improved seed varieties, fertilizers, insecticides and improved weeding – can usually be applied equally well and efficiently on small farms. Under conditions of abundant rural labour and continuous rapid population growth, productivity per unit of land will be the most relevant measure for policy purposes for the next several decades.[2] Obviously it is the purpose of economic development to raise labour's productivity – but not only among the few. In order to raise labour productivity broadly for all those now in farming and those yet to be absorbed by the agricultural sector, land and capital must be redistributed.

2. Actually, a single-factor productivity measure (such as land or labour) is not wholly adequate. What is needed is a measure of efficiency or productivity based on output per unit of total inputs with inputs valued at their social opportunity costs. Unfortunately, data are not available for the latter calculations.

A number of recent studies, comparing farm size and output per unit of land, support the hypothesis that output per unit of land is inversely related to farm size. Figure 1 (from Dorner and Kanel, 1971) presents graphically the results of these studies, most of which measure output in terms of gross value per unit of land. Value of output per unit of land above variable cost would be a better measure since it would minimize the distortions due to possible differences in amount of capital used by farms of different sizes. However, in those cases where such a concept was used, the results are consistent with the gross-value concept. In fact, using gross-value probably understates the small farm's margin over the large farm since small farms generally employ less capital.

Some may contend that these data do not *prove* an inverse relationship between farm size and productivity per unit of land. However, they do cast serious doubts upon the general presumption of a highly positive relationship which underlies most arguments against land reform in regions with a large-estate system.[3]

Notes to figure 1

1. [India] From data for the mid- and late-1950s gathered by the Studies in Economics of Farm Management, Ministry of Food and Agriculture, Government of India, New Delhi. Output as gross value in rupees per acre. Long classified actual farm sizes into four size-groups – smallest, second smallest, second largest, largest – for each of eight areas in seven states, and presented output per size group as the average of the eight areas. Data from more than 1000 farms from seven states (Long, 1961a).

2. [Brazil] Output as net sales per productive hectare, in thousands of cruzeiros (1963). Actual farm sizes included in each size class are: (a) 0–10 has.; (b) 10. 1–20 has.; (c) 20. 1–40 has.; (d) 40. 1–100 has.;

3. The studies summarized in Figure 1 are quite variable. Some use country census data, others are based on survey samples. The concept of 'small' farms and farm-size class varies widely, usually, however, reflecting the range of conditions encountered in the specific studies. These variations do not invalidate the general conclusions concerning an inverse relationship between farm size and output per unit of land. It is this general and consistent pattern which underlies the statement that these data cast doubt upon the widely held view of a positive relationship between farm size and output.

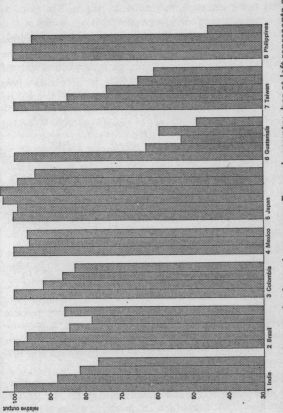

Figure 1 Output per hectare for farm size-groups. For each country, bar at left represents output per hectare for smallest farm size-group; bars to the right represent successively larger farms with their output per hectare expressed as a per cent of that of the smallest size-group.

(e) more than 100 has. Sample of 311 farms (Johnson and Buse, 1967).

3. [Colombia, 1950] Output as per cent of value of subfamily (smallest) farm production per cultivated hectare. The authors classed actual farm sizes into four groups: subfamily, family, multi-family medium, and multifamily large. Based on National Census data (Barraclough and Domike, 1966).

4. [Mexico, 1960] Output as gross value per hectare of arable land, in pesos. Actual farm sizes included in each size-class are: (a) less than 5 hectares in the private sector (average about 1·45 has.); (b) *ejido* lands averaging about 7 hectares per *ejido* member (only about 2 per cent of 1·6 million *ejido* members engage in collective farming); (c) more than 5 has. in the private sector (average about 27 has.). Based on National Census data (Dovring, 1969).

5. [Japan, 1960] The author uses data from the Japanese Farm Household Survey of 1960. Output as total receipts per *cho* minus fertilizer costs per *cho*, for seven crops. Farm sizes are classified into six groups: (a) less than 0·3 *cho*; (b) 0·3–0·5 *cho*; (c) 0·5–1·0 *cho*; (d) 1·0–1·5 *chos*; (e) 1·5–2·0 *chos*; (f) more than 2·0 *chos*. One *cho* is slightly larger than one hectare (USDA, 1965).

6. [Guatemala, 1950] Output as value product per utilized hectare for nine selected crops, in US dollars. Farms are classified into five groups; micro farms, subfamily, family, multifamily medium, and multifamily large (Comité Inter-americano de Desarrollo Agrícola, CIDA, 1965).

7. [Taiwan, 1965] Output as net farm income per *chia*, in thousand NT dollars. Actual farm sizes are: (a) under 0·51 *chia*; (b) 0·52–1·03 *chias*; (c) 1·04–1·54 *chias*; (d) 1·55–2·06 *chias*; (e) over 2·07 *chias*. One *chia* is 0·9699 hectare (Christensen, 1968).

8. [Philippines, 1963–4] Output in kilograms per hectare per year. Farms were placed in four groups: (a) below 1·0 ha.; (b) 1·1–2·0 has.; (c) 2·1–3·0 has.; (d) above 3·0 has. Figure depicts relative productivity for share tenants in Barrio Balatong B. (Ruttan, 1966).

In a Chilean study Morales (1964) analysed output per hectare for farm size-groups ranging from ten to 500 hectares of irrigated land. In this study, soil quality, distance to market, and even type of farming were held constant. Even under these rigidly controlled conditions, there were no statistically signifi-cant differences in output per hectare for farms in the various size-groups despite the fact that the small farms experienced greater difficulties in obtaining credit and water for irrigation.

The relationships shown in Figure 1 are cast in a static context. However, the relationships revealed are the end products of such dynamics as have existed in the society. In his analysis of Indian data, Long suggested that similar analysis from societies whose agriculture has been more dynamic might be more relevant. The data from Mexico, Taiwan and Japan are especially revealing in this regard. As Long (1961) points out,

if data for such countries [as Japan] reveal a negative relationship between size-of-farm and gross value productivity per acre above variable capital costs as the end result of a highly dynamic agricultural development process, then indeed the presuppositions of most land reform discussions – and also of much technical assistance work – need intense re-examination.

The data for Japan certainly are not inconsistent with this view. In fact the multiple cropping ratio (not shown in figure 1) is consistently smaller as farm size increases. In the case of Taiwan, Figure 1 shows a very consistent inverse relation between farm size and net farm income per unit of land. From 1940 to 1965, cultivated land per farm was reduced by almost one half while output per hectare *more than* doubled (Christensen, 1968, p. 40). The Mexican data also support this view. The *ejido* sector in 1960 had only about a quarter of the total land but accounted for a third of all marketed farm produce. In terms of sales as a per cent of total output, the *ejido* sector sold practically the same proportion (65·2) as did the large-farm sector (67·7) (Dovring, 1969).[4]

It might be argued that the higher productivity per unit of land on existing small farms is no real evidence that new units to be created by splitting up large farms would achieve increased productivity. But the evidence available on post-reform experiences – in Mexico, Bolivia, Japan, Taiwan, Yugoslavia, Egypt (Schmid, 1969) – shows that although in some cases there was an initial drop, average productivity per unit of land

4. The *ejido* sector did have a higher proportion of the arable land while the large-farm sector had more of the pasture land and produced most of the livestock for slaughter.

increased rather substantially after these reforms. All cases involved a reduction in the average size of farm.

These data and arguments are not presented to argue for small holdings *per se* or for a family-farm system. *Circumstances around the world are much too variable to permit any valid generalization with respect to the system of organization to be established in agriculture*. On the other hand, it is instructive to look closely at small farms since they now exist in most countries, and at least in some cases their number will likely increase as a result of land reforms. Also, most socialist systems allow a family-farm sector to co-exist with the larger cooperative enterprises, allocate private plots to families working in the cooperatives, or have individualized production combined with cooperative servicing and marketing. The main point to be emphasized is that development requires an agriculture organized in such a way as to: (a) assure incentives for productive work and investment, (b) use a combination of production factors consistent with the cost and availability of these factors at a given time, and (c) provide an equitable distribution of the increased output.

At present, active government involvement in the process of economic development tends to favour large production units. They have better and earlier access to improved technology, to credit, and to markets. But with the availability of an infrastructure and of cooperative and public service organizations that do not discriminate against them, the advantage often shifts to family farms (Kanel, 1971).

A good example of such a shift is found in the evolution of Danish agriculture, especially in the role of large farms and of peasants in the manufacture of butter (Skrubbeltrang, 1953). Early in the nineteenth century peasants were given personal freedom and ownership of the plots they worked, but the landed aristocracy retained large portions of their former estates. In the immediate post-reform era the large farms made the best quality butter, largely because they could afford the facilities for on-the-farm cooling of milk. This technological advantage compensated for the difficulties of supervising hired labour. By the end of the century the situation was reversed because of technological and institutional changes – the invention of the centrifugal cream separator, and the emergence of a strong cooperative movement, including cooperative creameries, which had the necessary facilities for cooling the cream and making high quality butter. These two changes permitted the small farmers to separate and deliver the concentrated cream to the creameries instead of having to ship the bulkier milk or to make butter at home. The cooperatives were quality and market conscious (a major market outlet was exports to England, and quality was extremely important), and they were effective in influencing production practices on the farms which improved quality of the cream. In consequence, small farms gained a competitive advantage over large farms; both had more or less equal access to improved technology, yet large farms were at a relative disadvantage due to higher labour costs and the difficulties in supervising labour (Kanel, 1971).

A final case of interest is reported by Dovring for pre-Second World War Hungary. Data for the period 1929–38 show that not only were the smallest farms producing almost twice as much per unit of land as the large farms, but they also marketed more. Although the large farms sold a greater proportion of their total output, the small farms produced enough per unit of land to sell about 40 per cent more product per unit of land (measured in value terms) than did the large farms. 'Thus the small farms were by no means disconnected from the market; they even made a proportionately greater contribution to market supplies than the larger farms' (Dovring, 1970, p. 13).

The evidence seems quite clear that small farms, either co-existing with large farms within a pre-reform dual system or operating as the end product of a distributive reform, have a better performance record of output per unit of land than do large estates. Again, the reforms that establish state farms and collectives are difficult to evaluate within this framework. As with the employment question – it depends. It depends on the particular priority and emphasis given to agricultural development. The large-unit (state and collective farms) system of Russia has not performed too well, but its defects seem more directly related to deliberate policy decisions concerning investment priorities between industry and agriculture (and the mechanization emphasis within parts of agriculture) than to a lack of productive response to the investments made.

Agriculture's contribution to capital formation in other sectors

One other issue, the contribution of the agricultural sector to investments in the rest of the economy, and the influence of land tenure reforms in affecting such capital transfers, demands comment. As mentioned earlier, landowners who have the ability to evaluate investment alternatives may find the more profitable ones in sectors other than agriculture. How well such investments will serve the overall requirements of a nation's development efforts is not clear. Many of the investment needs are for social overhead or of a scale requirement that call for a pooling of capital difficult to achieve in the absence of well organized financial markets.

In all cases of developing countries today, there is need for a large scale *public* investment programme; *governments* must gain access to a substantial pool of investment funds. In those countries where the agricultural sector is large relative to the total economy, agriculture must be a major source of savings. In simple physical terms, agriculture must provide food for the people released from the agricultural sector who are now engaged in building capital structures – roads, schools, factories, canals, etc. Since these investments do not have a quick payoff, agriculture must, so to speak, donate part of this food without an equivalent short-term return. Owen has stated the question: 'How can peasants be encouraged to produce a cumulative surplus of food and fibre over and above their own consumption, and how can this surplus largely be channelled to investment activity in the non-farm sector without requiring in exchange an equivalent transfer of productive value to the farm sector?' (Owen, 1966, pp. 43–4).

Even in the US, Owen estimates that this production squeeze was between $1·5 and $2 billion in 1960. Raup (1960) points out that among the industrialized nations,

those countries in which agriculture is well rewarded have made much slower rates of economic growth in the twentieth century. France is an outstanding example. England belongs in this class.

So do Sweden and the low countries of Europe generally. [He also suggests that] capital formation in postwar Germany has again been accomplished in part because of the 'tribute' laid on its agriculture in the form of lower rewards than those available in industrial occupations (pp. 317–18).

This squeeze on agriculture, according to Owen, (1966) is a feature of all developing societies, whether socialist or capitalist.

The difference between the Russian and US approaches to development lies not in the fact that one exacted or exacts a special contribution from the farmers and the other did, or does, not. Rather the difference lies in the way in which the squeeze has been applied and in the relative efficiency with which the process has operated in each case (p. 44).

This concept of a squeeze on agriculture presents a dilemma of contradictory requirements. Investments in agriculture must be made and agricultural productivity must increase, but at the same time the terms of trade must be kept somewhat unfavourable to agriculture (Mellor, 1966). The latter requirement is inconsistent with the recommendation of many economists for increasing farm prices to encourage investments. As pointed out earlier, land tenure institutions are significant here in that they determine who controls the investment decisions.

Thus at times, especially in the early phases of industrialization, there is need for a substantial net capital flow from agriculture to other sectors. Yet, this squeeze on agriculture cannot continue indefinitely; it must be accompanied by public investments designed to improve the conditions of life and to increase productivity in the farm sector. Government policies must be designed for extracting an investible surplus *from* agriculture while at the same time providing for public investments *in* the agricultural sector – for transportation, marketing, communication and education systems, and for credit, health, research and extension services.

Tenure institutions are important because it is often the landlords who extract the surplus from the peasants. If landowners are also very influential in government, there is no public power to get the surplus away from them, and decisions on investing it rest with the landowning class. Investments guided by their private interests are not necessarily consistent with those required for developing the country.

Though the efficiency of taxing many small landowners is sometimes questioned, Eckstein reminds us that

while administratively it may be easier to collect taxes from a small number of landlords than from a numerous peasantry, politically just the reverse may be true. Actually land reform may serve as one of the means by which it becomes politically feasible to transfer the accumulating function from the landlord to the state (Eckstein, 1955, p. 660, quoted by Raup, 1967, p. 279).

Specific instances of this 'squeeze on agriculture' are again apparent in various reform experiences. In Russia, the large landlords' estates as well as many of the larger peasant holdings were eliminated by the land reapportionment of 1917–18 and by the class war in the villages of 1918–20. Yet ten years later, in 1928, the decision was taken to collectivize Soviet agriculture (Nove, 1971). Evidently, an individualistic farm sector represented certain political threats to the communist party leadership. But there was also an underlying economic rationale. The magnitude of the surplus that had to be extracted from agriculture in order to support the massive industrialization efforts which the Soviet leaders set as their goal could not be obtained under a system with an independent peasantry. Under conditions of individual farming, the government could not have restricted consumption to the same extent as it did via the collective and state farms (Schiller, 1971).

Platt's discussion of land reform in the United Arab Republic mentions a frustration of the middle class because of generally negative attitudes in the landlord-dominated Parliament toward social and tax legislation.

The reluctance of Parliament to tax the great landed wealth of the countryside limited government revenues to 5 per cent of national income, giving scant funds for public projects. . . . [Later Platt notes that] whereas in pre-reform days the landlord class drained capital away from the rural area and spent it on luxury living featuring much import buying and travel abroad, or in buying more land, the post-reform increase in peasant income has been nearly all spent locally. This spending has supported domestic industry and trade in textiles, housewares, farm implements, and other basics contributory to the internal economy, and has cut down the flow of funds away from the land and out of the country (Platt, 1970, p. 59).

Voelkner points out that the earlier Japanese reforms of the 1870s attempted to enhance the government's ability to collect more taxes from the rural sector. All available surplus was to be squeezed from farm production. And indeed during the 1880s and 1890s, the Japanese land tax provided 80 per cent or more of all tax revenue.

Apparently the heavy squeeze on agriculture to finance early development did pay off. Japanese agricultural and industrial development was rapid during the time between the first land reform in 1870 and the First World War. Neither did agriculture lose all these syphoned-off surpluses. Japanese infrastructure which heavily benefited agriculture was mostly constructed during this period (Voelkner, 1970, p. 53; see also Dore, 1959).

Speaking of the Mexican case, Flores (1971) writes:

The fact remains that between 1910 and 1941 no foreign capital entered Mexico. On the contrary, wealthy Mexicans with liquid capital sent it abroad and thereby aggravated the balance-of-payments deficit. There were, therefore, only two ways to increase the domestic rate of capital formation: (a) the classic, painful, and expedient recourse of squeezing agriculture as much as possible; and (b) the more enterprising transfer of workers from agriculture to the emerging industrial and urban sectors, and their employment at subsistence wages in activities which would eventually increase the productive capacity of the system. This is how public works were financed and how huge government deficits were covered until 1942. This explains largely the paradox of the success and failure of Mexican agriculture: the penury of the peasants and slum dwellers and the impressive agricultural, industrial, and urban growth (p. 518).

Taiwan's reform once again presents an interesting case. In the pre-reform period, 1926–40, per hectare yields of rice increased 1·4 per cent annually, land rents increased 1·2 per cent annually, and the value of paddy land (in terms of paddy rice) increased 2·0 per cent annually (Koo, 1970, p. 12). Therefore, it was essentially the landlords who were benefiting both through land-value increases and rent increases. How or even whether they invested this 'surplus' cannot be determined.

In addition to rental payments, however, funds flowed out of Taiwan's agriculture through payments of farmers for interest, taxes and fees; through savings deposits by farmers in financial institutions; and through relative shifts in the terms of trade between agricultural products and those products farmers bought from other sectors. Lee has estimated the net real outflow of capital from Taiwan's agricultural sector for 1920, 1940 and 1960 to be 64, 51, and 100 million Taiwan dollars, respectively, at constant (1934–7) prices (Christensen, 1968, p. 25, quoting from Lee, 1967).

In reviewing the period 1895–1960, Lee distinguishes between financial, or visible, flows and invisible flows – the latter resulting from changes in the terms of trade. Financially, transfers through land-rent payments and government taxation were most important in the pre-Second World War period, while transfers in the form of farmers' savings became increasingly important in the postwar period. Invisible real net capital outflows brought about by terms of trade unfavourable to agriculture were less important in the prewar period but accounted for more than 50 per cent of the total outflow in the postwar years. Throughout this entire 1895–1960 period, there was a net capital outflow from Taiwan's agricultural sector. The magnitude of this outflow showed a roughly increasing trend until near the end of the period (Lee, 1968).

Land reform also has impacts on investments in local services – education, health, recreation, transport, welfare, etc. A landlord-dominated economy usually provides for a separate system of these services to serve only the elite (Dorner and Felstehausen, 1970). Again the experience of Taiwan is instructive. Farm families, following the land reform, apparently used a substantial part of their increased incomes to educate their children. The percentage of primary school-age children in school increased from 71 per cent in 1940 to 96 per cent in 1960 (Christensen, 1968, p. 48, and Koo, 1970, p. 61).

Frequently, landlords living in cities or towns have no interest in taxing themselves to provide for services in both the cities of their residence *and* in the rural communities. Raup (1967) has summarized this point:

Weak government in underdeveloped regions is often associated with poor quality education, public health services, police protection, and roads. Fundamental to this weakness is the lack of a local tax base. With semisubsistence production and primitive levels of trade, the most feasible base for local taxation is land and natural resources. This introduces one of the most serious handicaps to development – the inadequacy of land and property tax systems. Land tenure structures are often responsible for this inadequacy (p. 278).

This taxing inadequacy is a very serious shortcoming, and it continues to plague some of the industrialized nations. Writing about the US South, Nicholls places the blame for the low level of average years of schooling completed by the Negro farm population squarely on the large landowners.

In striking contrast to most of the Middle West, the South has been dominated by power groups who, shunning the public schools in the education of their own children, see little reason to tax themselves in order to finance the education of the less privileged classes (Nicholls, 1960, pp. 110–13, quoted in Thiesenhusen, 1969, p. 744).

The ability to create a tax structure with which to finance an investment programme for uplifting the quality of life in the countryside is an important aspect of development policy. This ability frequently hinges on the type and nature of land tenure institutions. Over time, and with productivity increasing at a sufficiently rapid rate, the needed investments can be made in the agricultural sector and, additionally, a net investible surplus can be obtained from agriculture for capital formation in other sectors. Without increases in productivity, however, squeezing a surplus from agriculture becomes a process of peasant exploitation – either by powerful landowners or by the state. In many of the agrarian countries today, development policies are difficult to implement as a result of a long history of peasant exploitation.

6 Needed Redirections in Analyses and in Policies

Have the poor people of the world benefited from the development strategies of the past several decades? In an absolute sense, and on the average, there may have been a slight improvement. But the number of poor have increased and inequalities have mounted. There has been considerable economic growth but, paradoxically, little development. Under present agrarian structures existing in many countries, it is difficult to visualize the needed achievements in: increased total farm output and productivity; higher incomes for the large mass of rural poor people; expanded employment opportunities for a rapidly growing labour force; and incorporation of the peasant into the mainstream of the nation's economic and political life.

Without strong rural organizations pressuring for change, there is little incentive for redistribution and a widening of opportunities (Powell, 1971). People in power do not, without compelling reasons, initiate action which deprives them of special privileges. The basic dilemma is that a major investment programme in human and material resources creating an opportunity-oriented system reduces the short-run advantage and privilege of the favoured groups, whereas a system built on inequality and privilege is inconsistent with economic development.

Programmes designed to increase agricultural productivity are often conceived and organized in national capitals and administered through a hierarchical bureaucratic organization. There is often a complete absence of organizations in the countryside to serve peasants in channelling their expressed needs and grievances through government departments, in pressuring administrators of government programmes, and in influencing legislation. As a consequence, communication from peasants to government employees, and from lower-level civil servants to those in higher positions within the bureaucracy is often lacking.

Absence of alternative employment opportunities for government technicians may restrict the two-way communication process. Technicians may be less willing to propose changes if they believe their opinions contradict the positions held by their administrative superiors since incurring the disfavour of superiors is to run the risk of being without a job. Furthermore, technicians come largely from urban families or from land-owning classes and often fail to understand the culture and the problems of the peasants. Finally, there may be too much emphasis on ideology – on form rather than substance – in the policy implementation process. A policy to establish cooperatives may be deemed good in itself, and the bureaucratic effort may end once the cooperative has been 'established'; the ideological dictate is fulfilled. All these influences may restrict two-way communication (Dorner *et al.*, 1965).

Technicians at the several levels of bureaucracy frequently have few opportunities to exercise decision-making authority in interpreting policy and adjusting it to local circumstances. Yet such authority is necessary if policy is to meet the needs of special cases (which often means most cases). Legislation, no matter how wisely conceived and well planned, cannot possibly anticipate all the consequences of its implementation or identify all the special situations to which it must apply. Peasant organizations, if they are independently created by peasants to represent their interests, can serve as vehicles for communicating with and pressuring governments whenever programmes do not fit their needs or are creating difficulties for them.

The energizing force in the development process is not provided solely or even primarily by the investment plans and projects of administrators and entrepreneurs. The informed self-interest of farmers and urban workers and their creative human energies are strategic to any long-term development effort. While authoritarian measures can carry development to a certain stage, it is the mass of common people who must provide the energy and the markets to keep the process going. This requires widely shared economic and political citizenship which can be realized only through basic reforms and the reallocation of power.

Many arguments against reform and redistribution are rooted in philosophical-ideological concepts based on the nature of, and the rights vested in, private property. Such arguments, not surprisingly, are most frequently presented by large landowners and people representing their interests. Some even claim that private property is a right ordained by natural law and that any attack on it is an attack on the basic unit of society – the family. Private property, it is claimed, is a pillar of civilization. If this premise is accepted, then it must be admitted that property cannot perform these laudible functions if most people are without it. The logic of this argument suggests a wider distribution of property – not a condition where the mass of people are deprived of it.

What is often overlooked, even by less dogmatic adherents to the concept, is that private property cannot exist without an organization to protect it and enforce the rules. In the absence of nation states, for example, feudal lords had to have their own army to protect their 'property'. Private property does not imply absolute rights; all nations place many restrictions on it, and the state reserves the right to alter the rules in the future.

Private property, freedom of contract, and competition may well serve to accentuate existing inequalities. These institutional forms have far different consequences in an open, mobile society with alternatives widely recognized and available than they do in a class structured, immobile society with alternatives greatly restricted. The survival and effective functioning of these institutional forms rests on the freedom and flexibility within a political system that permits the emergence of organizations and pressure groups as natural outgrowths of commonly recognized and shared interests. Without such organizations, without a multitude of interests pressuring governmental officials, who is to say what constitutes the *public* interest? In the absence of such pressures, government policies may serve only the interests of the few.

While reform of the land tenure system may restrict private property rights and freedom of enterprise when judged by the rules under which these institutions operate in a pre-reform setting, distributive reforms are not inconsistent with these institutions under a new set of rules with a redistribution of power. The fact of the matter is that these institutions frequently do not perform in the interests of the majority of the people. They cannot perform in the public interest until there is a more equal distribution of wealth, power and opportunity.

Of course, there is no reason to assume that nations will choose a post-reform system based on private property in land. Under conditions existing in the less-industrialized countries today, major reforms will often lead to mixed systems of private, state and cooperative enterprises in the agricultural sector. These issues must be worked out by the people of each country.

The successes and difficulties of land reforms or attempted reforms, the influence of national and local contexts, and the multiple problems but also the potential benefits of redistributive reform policies were illustrated, largely through case studies, in preceding chapters. Several suggestions concerning changes that could be made in the international sphere are outlined below. These suggestions rest on several premises.

Firstly, governments everywhere represent a variety of interests – there is no homogeneous, monolithic view on such fundamental policy issues as that represented by land reform and development policies and strategies. Minority positions become those of the majority, sometimes over a short period of time. There is always diversity and conflict, situations in many countries are relatively fluid, and new alignments of power sometimes emerge very rapidly. Secondly, the fundamental development issues are not only economic, social and political. They are intellectual issues as well. The assumptions and preconceptions underlying development plans and policies, and the criteria of evaluation employed in setting priorities, are among the intellectual components having a profound influence on the way the task of development is conceptualized.

The role of international agencies and organizations

The appropriate role of international agencies in dealing with these complex issues must be reconsidered, especially that of the United Nations and its specialized agencies. A long series of UN agreements, reports and declarations, most recently the resolution on social progress and development approved by the General Assembly in 1969, make a strong plea for 'participation of all members of society in productive and socially useful labour' and the establishment of 'forms of ownership of land and of the means of production which preclude any kind of exploitation of man, ensure equal rights to property for all and create conditions leading to genuine equality among people.'

Likewise, in 1961 representatives of the governments of the Americas established the Alliance for Progress and pledged themselves 'to encourage, in accordance with the characteristics of each country, programs of comprehensive agrarian reforms leading to the effective transformation, where required, of unjust structures and systems of land tenure.' Signatories to these and other pronouncements were heads of nation states or their designated representatives. Did they not believe in the principles espoused by these declarations? Or did they personally believe in these principles but find political opposition at home too strong to implement policies consistent with their convictions?

Of course the world is a long way from an international political authority and mechanisms whereby the policies of nation states can be significantly influenced. Indeed, among the principles of international organization are those proclaiming the right and responsibility of member states to determine freely their own destiny without external interference. However, if self-determination does not conform, at least in broad outline, to the principles of the United Nations Charter and the subsequent declarations and conventions, then the enshrinement of such principles in instruments entered into by the participating countries is quite pointless (FAO Report, 1971).

At a minimum, it would seem, the United Nations and its agencies must speak out vigorously on these topics and on the principles which have been accepted regardless of what individual governments may say or do. They must also revise present priorities in providing technical and financial assistance. The Food and Agricultural Organization of the United

Nations has an important role in land reform, yet this very large agency, with a bureaucracy at the Rome headquarters and in the field numbering in the thousands, has but a modest section and field staff devoted to land reform. Land reform remains somewhat of an *ad hoc* activity within this large bureaucracy. Although here too there have been many pronouncements about land reform, these pronouncements have not permeated the practice and operating philosophy of this agency. The same might be said of the World Bank and some of the regional banks as well. Lip service is sometimes given to land reform, employment and distributional issues, but the money frequently flows in directions quite inconsistent with these objectives.

Needed redirections in analyses

Why are policies not formulated to accommodate the several key objectives and requirements of development – increased output, increased employment, and a more equitable distribution of income? The distributional questions, of course, raise many tough political issues. Accordingly, and regretfully, policy recommendations of professional analysts using highly sophisticated models usually ignore employment and distributional aspects. Development planning and project evaluation is conceived as a calculation of benefits and costs *within* the present structure of income distribution. Recommendations are too often based on private or project decision-making criteria rather than those appropriate to the interests of the entire nation.

Three basic assumptions underlying much of the present analyses of agricultural development planning allow certain strategic developmental imperatives to fall between the analytical slats. These assumptions concern the creation of secure opportunities on the land; the development of human abilities and capacities; and the inclusion of income distribution as an explicit variable in the analysis (Dorner, 1971b).

Creation of secure opportunities on the land

The 'war on hunger' position tends to assume that if there are hungry people, food should be produced by the cheapest, most efficient means possible. Yet frequently, and especially when viewed from the private interest of an individual firm, this efficiency includes displacing people with machines.

It has become an article of faith among many professionals that mechanization always creates as many jobs as it destroys, sometimes more. According to this assumption, there may indeed be some short-run problems of labour displacement and some temporary unemployment. But given time, the new technology creates demand for labour in many other areas of the economy through its various linkages, and eventually employment will rise to a higher level.

This assumption may be justified in a highly industrialized nation. But does the same assumption apply to a country that does not produce its own machines? In the United States, for example, the mechanical cotton picker displaced workers by the tens of thousands. Many of the workers displaced (though certainly not all) and especially their children did find employment among the complex of industries involved in the production, sale and servicing of cotton pickers – steel, rubber, oil, machinery manufacture, transport, farm implement sales and service, etc. But what about Nicaragua, which imports cotton pickers from the United States? Most of the industries linked with the cotton picker do not exist in Nicaragua; they remain in the United States.

The manager of a large farm enterprise may find the importation of such machines highly profitable due to a variety of circumstances, many of them related to government policies: overvalued exchange rates, special import privileges, subsidized credit, etc. Current United States and European experience with farm enlargement is sometimes cited to justify this mechanization emphasis. But such an analogy is inappropriate given the widely different situation with respect to the relative abundance of capital and labour in the United States and Europe as compared with the developing world. The *real* costs of capital and labour in these nations (in contrast to existing prices which are often distorted by the above mentioned policies) differ widely from those in the industrial nations.

The cotton picker case illustrates the general principle involved; it does not argue against all modern, imported technology. In mechanization, much depends on what the machines will be used for. In an agriculture with an overabundant and growing labour supply, however, it is unlikely that one can make a case for importation of most machines that are primarily labour-saving rather than output increasing if the problem is viewed from the standpoint of national development rather than profit maximization of the private firm.

Even with low wages there is a strong incentive on large farms to mechanize and thus simplify labour supervision. It is almost impossible to find farms of, say, 1000 hectares in rice or cotton that are planted, tended and harvested mainly by large crews of wage labour. These farms either mechanize or operate with a share-cropper system.

To get at the crux of the matter, policies specifically intended to achieve *both* increases in agricultural production and increases in employment with a more equitable income distribution *must* provide the large mass of rural families with *secure opportunities on the land*. Land tenure institutions and size of holdings must be specifically included as variables in economic analysis. But the basic assumptions underlying economic theories of production and distribution take these as 'givens'.

Development of human abilities and capacities

Another aspect of the employment issue which receives little attention is that of improving the productive capacity of labour. Potentially, the most abundant resource is labour – *potentially* since transforming raw labour into manpower resources needed for development (with skills, experiences and discipline) requires both formal training and work experience. The scarcest resource generally is capital. Given the abundance of people, there has been a tendency to ignore the need for investment in their development. Instead of viewing land as a vehicle for employing people and for developing the skills and experience required by the rural labour force, land has been viewed primarily as a resource to be efficiently combined with scarce capital so as to maximize agricultural output.

Of course, many poor countries have not been able to supply even elementary schooling for large numbers of their people.

Still, formal schooling is not the only and not always the most significant dimension in the development of the human labour potential. Economic activity must be and can be designed to produce educational effects. Productive work can offer an educational experience and a discipline as valid as that gained in the classroom.

The manner in which increased production is achieved, and the number of people who participate and reap benefits from the experience, may be as important as the production increase itself. One gets a different perspective regarding the role of land if (in addition to its accepted function as a factor in the production of farm products) it is viewed as a vehicle both for creating economic opportunities and for upgrading the quality, skills and capacities of the mass of rural people.

Man is a resource to be used (along with land and capital) as well as the user of resources. An individual plays a dual role – he is both the user and the used, the interested and the object of interest, the exploiter and the exploited.

In a society where economic and political power are widely shared, there is a continuous attempt to modify institutional structures in order to keep this process of 'using others' mutually beneficial. Procedures are designed so that individuals and groups, in pursuing their private interests, are not injuring (preferably, are furthering) the interests of other individuals and groups. When mutuality in the process breaks down and conflicts intensify, zones of discretional behaviour of the individuals and groups involved must be redefined in order to re-establish mutuality in the processes of associated living.

Economic efficiency models commonly view man as labour power – as an object of use. This view accepts the *status quo* power position and ownership pattern of land and capital. In fact, it places the weight of 'scientific analysis' in the camp of present owners. Under conditions of vast and increasing inequality, policy prescriptions based on such models are consistent with the poor man's view of the world: 'Them that has – gets.'

Inclusion of income distribution as a variable in analyses

Economists tend to de-emphasize the income distribution consequences of the development process. Since land tenure arrangements are most directly associated with the creation of and access to income-earning opportunities, they receive only passing mention in the literature on agricultural development.

If the task of development is conceptualized to include income distribution as a variable, some of the economists' most powerful ideas and tools lose much of their analytical leverage. For example, marginal analysis and the accompanying planning, programming, and budgeting tools implicitly assume certain stable parameters, e.g. a given and unchanging income distribution. Yet once an elaborate and somewhat arbitrary measurement emerges, as from benefit–cost analysis, a strong faith is placed in it. The unstated implicit assumptions remain unstated and are frequently ignored. The higher the benefit-cost ratio, the 'better' the project.

However, the results of such calculations are directly conditioned by the pattern of income distribution. Investments in the increased production of chickens and beans rather than airlines and television sets might give a good benefit–cost ratio if the pattern of income distribution were changed. Poor people, lacking the money votes, cannot register their needs or desires in the market. But change the income distribution and you change the structure of demand, thus changing the benefit–cost ratios of various projects which in turn alter investment priorities.

It is often said that the objectives of equity and productivity are in conflict. Yet the evidence summarized in preceding chapters supports the opposite conclusion – the social and political goals of wider distribution of opportunity, power and employment among farm people are *not* in conflict with increased agricultural productivity and efficiency. The dilemma of the hard choices countries must make – between distributive justice and economic efficiency or advancement – is not a real issue.[1] Equity and productivity goals conflict only if the present

1. Whether or not a major conflict between distributive justice and economic efficiency is considered an important issue depends on the time

ownership structure of land and capital is assumed to be fixed. Or put another way, they may present conflicting demands for the owner of a large estate based on calculations for his private account, but these conflicts are not in evidence when calculations are based on a national account (if all social costs and benefits are entered in the calculations). The significant distributional questions are not those defined by marginal productivity theory, but those inherent in the existing economic and political power and the patterns of resource ownership, use and control to which they give rise.

This issue has been succinctly stated by Long (1952):

Distribution theory today concerns itself, in essence, with tracing out the effects of various policies in distributing economic fruits among persons who own or otherwise command control over resources. . . . In current theory, distribution of ownership or other control of resources among people is 'given'. . . . In terms of the dynamics of economic development, however, the real problem of distribution is: 'How does ownership or other control over resources come to be distributed in the manner it is?' . . . The question is not, for example, whether a landlord and a tenant each receives the appropriate return for the resources he controls; but rather, is it appropriate, from the standpoint of the economic development of the country in question, for the landlord and the tenant to have these particular proportions of the nation's resources under his control (pp. 729–30).

Falcon notes the 'powerful forces that are pressing for mechanization of all kinds. Large farmers, foreign and domestic industrialists, politicians and even aid agencies have vested interests in promoting various implements, including tractors' (Falcon, 1970, p. 706). He then documents a number of examples of World Bank loans for these purposes, and World Bank mechanization loans are not unique. Much of the international capital assistance for the improvement of agriculture in the less-developed countries has benefited primarily the

---

dimension within which development is conceived. The dilemma of the hard choices may indeed be a real one if development is viewed within a very short time horizon. Such a short-run view is understandable in the case of individuals. A nation's development policies, however, *must* take the long view.

large farmer and the more privileged in the agricultural sectors of these countries. This concentration of benefits reflects not only the policy of international agencies and banks but also the internal policies of developing nations and political power of those for whom mechanization (and related investments) is a profitable venture – profitable, that is, by criteria appropriate to the individual firm but inappropriate to national development. These policies of international lending agencies and of nation states – both the more and the less developed – also reflect the way in which many economists view the development task, since economists provide many of the analyses on which such policies are based.

An analysis of the United States aid programme to Latin American agriculture concluded that only about 10 per cent of all United States assistance in the period 1962–8 was specifically earmarked for agriculture. Of this total, over 50 per cent was classified as benefiting primarily commercial farmers. Only 15 per cent was aimed directly at agrarian reform or the beneficiaries of reform programmes. The remaining 35 per cent was for general improvements likely to benefit both large and small farms (Davis, 1970). The record of United States aid to Latin America on this score is perhaps not worse, is perhaps even better, than that of most multi- or bilateral assistance programmes during this same period.

International and bilateral assistance agencies could influence, in many ways, the consequences of their assistance and ensure that their efforts are not working against the urgent requirements to create more jobs, improve income distribution, and elevate the conditions of life of the mass of people at the bottom of the present income distribution pyramids. They could encourage recipient governments to allow free association and organization of rural workers, sharecroppers, tenants and small owners and to make every effort to support and strengthen these organizations and to work more closely with them.[2] In considering various projects for which technical and

2. International and national aid-giving agencies of course face many problems. In theory at least, such agencies cannot go 'over the heads' of national governments to reach and influence directly the people in the receiving country. Yet in fact aid directed at helping the underprivileged

financial assistance are requested, these agencies should give preference to those which involve changes in the tenure structure and which hold promise for benefiting the large mass of rural people rather than the privileged few. The social, employment and income distribution effects of development projects should be accorded equal weight *vis-à-vis* the other variables in conventional benefit–cost calculations. And finally, assistance could be withheld from projects likely to lead to increased concentration of wealth and income and to greater social inequality. Such steps, however, require a change in the basic assumptions underlying the conceptualization of the development task, and a rejection of the idea that economic growth is synonymous with or inevitably leads to development in its broader meanings and dimensions.

Changing the paradigm of the international economic order

Green points out that many problems in the international economic sphere have been attacked and some more or less successfully resolved. But these, he notes, have been the problems affecting primarily the industrial countries, not the less-developed ones – massive credits for preventing monetary instability, but inability to raise much needed funds for soft loan-money for the World Bank's I D A (International Development Association); substantial progress in achieving international monetary reforms but lack of progress in devising ways and means of halting the erosion of the terms of trade for primary goods exports; creation of restrictive textile agreements but lack of sanctions on dumping farm surpluses; etc. (Green, 1970).

The resolution of these issues has benefited the industrial economies (with some secondary gains for the less-developed nations), but the obligations and costs have fallen on all, with the major burden often borne by the less-developed countries. Solution of unresolved international economic issues (e.g. the industrial nations' trade and market policies, which frequently prevent developing countries from taking full advantage either

---

will often fail to achieve its intended objectives unless some of these governments are themselves basically altered. Land reform gets 'hung-up' on these issues.

of static or dynamic comparative advantage) would favour the less-developed countries. In the resolution of these issues, however, costs would fall more heavily on the industrial economies. 'The basis for problem selection and resolution could hardly be more glaringly biased were it designed to impede development' (Green, 1970, p. 8).

One need not seek explanations for these phenomena in a devil theory of causation. These outcomes are much too complex to be explained by a theory of conspiracy and too well managed to be attributed to blind market forces. 'The problems of central concern to the metropolitan economies are the ones they (those who manage the world economic system, including the European socialist subsystem) readily see and understand as affecting them and for which they are trained and attuned to finding solutions' (Green, 1970, p. 8).

The intellectual paradigm of the international economic order influences their thinking. The record of the International Monetary Fund in Latin America and the World Bank's export development advice 'can only be explained rationally in this context – it does not stem either from malevolence or stupidity' (Green, 1970, p. 8).[3]

The analyst can help politicians and practitioners.

if he refrains from trying to adapt uncritically models and measures designed in and for industrial countries, where priorities are different, but helps instead to develop policies, national and international, to mitigate the great social problems of the Third World. . . . above all, the aim must be to change international attitudes so that it becomes impossible for political leaders and social scientists of Europe and North America to continue overlooking, and aggravating, often inadvertently, the obscene inequalities that disfigure the world (Seers, 1969, p. 6).

Needed redirections in policies

Massive land redistributions may not be politically feasible in all cases, but this does not mean that nothing can be done to

3. It should be acknowledged, however, that the outlook and policy directions of some of these agencies are changing. For example, the World Bank is becoming increasingly sensitive to the unemployment issue and is trying to develop ways of including job-creating criteria in its project evaluation procedures.

improve upon past performance. Special programmes can be devised to help producers in the small-farm areas. There is an urgent need to redirect governmental and commercial services – technical assistance, credit, marketing – to the needs of the small-farm sector. Such redirections will be needed in any event following a distributive land reform, but they can also play a critical role in developing the economic and political influence of the peasant subsector (Dorner and Felstehausen, 1970). If redistribution of land is not politically feasible in a particular country at a given point in time, it may at least be possible for such redirections in policy to be achieved, *especially if the capital and technical assistance of the international agencies is directed specifically to these purposes*. This would over time strengthen the economic and political power of the small-farm sector and provide it with the means to press for additional developmental changes – including the more wide-spread land redistribution measures required.

While industrialists have traditionally found common cause with the large landowners in opposing land reform, it is conceivable that increased income and purchasing power in the small-farm subsector will stimulate manufacturers of simple consumer goods to support the existing loose coalition favouring reform which exists in many countries – intellectuals, students, some sections of the governmental bureaucracy, left-of-centre military factions, and at times liberal elements within religious organizations (Thiesenhusen, 1970). Industries producing consumer goods for the domestic market may find it in their interest to raise the standard of living and the buying power of the peasantry (Kautsky, 1962).

It is possible, as Thiesenhusen (1970) concludes, that simple consumer goods and farm-input manufacturers would be joined by a broader cross-section of the urban middle class who see rapid migration to cities and its concomitants – increasing unemployment, political malaise, overcrowding, and higher city budgets – as a collective threat. This array of forces might be adequate to swing the balance of power away from the landlords allied with other conservative elements, among which are the protected 'advanced' industrialists. The power of the latter group, however, should not be underestimated.

Its interests are interlocked with landlords in a variety of ways. In some cases, it depends on landlords for foreign exchange. It may be bound to agriculture by family ties; this sector also tends to be associated with powerful foreign interests.

As stated several times in this text, land reform by itself does not offer solutions for all the complex issues of economic development. Neither does any other single measure. There are no quick, simple solutions. Land reform implies certain risks and costs, but present circumstances are not cost- and risk-free. Given a continuation of the development strategies of the past several decades – emphasizing investments and rates of return within existing institutional structures and de-emphasizing or even ignoring the questions of distribution and social justice – the prospects of world peace are not promising. A redirection of thought, analysis and action by policy makers, intellectuals and technicians working on the issues of development is imperative.

References

AHMAD, Z., and STERNBERG, M. J. (1971), 'Agrarian reform and employment, with special reference to Asia', *Agrarian Reform and Employment*, International Labour Office.

BAIROCH, P. (1964), *Révolution Industrielle et Sous-Développement*, Société d'édition d'enseignement superieur.

BARKER, R. (1970), 'Green revolution', *Current Affairs Bull.*, vol. 45, pp. 66–79.

BARRACLOUGH, S., and DOMIKE, A. (1966), 'Agrarian structure in seven Latin American countries', *Land Econ.*, vol. 42, pp. 391–424.

BARRACLOUGH, S., and SCHATAN, J. (1970), 'Technological policy and agricultural development', *Land Econ.*, forthcoming.

BREWSTER, J. (1950), 'The machine process in agriculture and industry', *J. of Farm Econ.*, vol. 32, pp. 69–81.

BROWN, L. R. (1970), *Seeds of Change*, Praeger.

BROWN, M. (1971a), 'Peasant organizations as vehicles of reform', in P. Dorner (ed.), *Land Reform in Latin America: Issues and Cases*, Land Economics Monograph no. 3.

BROWN, M. (1971b), 'Private efforts at reform', in P. Dorner (ed.), *Land Reform in Latin America: Issues and Cases*, Land Economics Monograph no. 3.

BURKE, M. (1970), 'Land reform and its effects upon production and productivity in the Lake Titicaca region', *Economic Development and Cultural Change*, vol. 18, pp. 410–50.

CARROLL, T. F. (1964), 'Reflexiones sobre la distribución del ingreso y la inversión agrícola', *Temas del BID*, Año 1, pp. 19–40.

CENTRAL STATISTICAL BOARD (1970), *Statistical Pocket Book of the Socialist Republic of Rumania*.

CÉPÈDE, M. (1971), 'The family farm: a primary unit of rural development in developing countries', in R. Weitz (ed.), *Rural Development in a Changing World*, MIT Press.

CHENG, C. (1970), 'Multiple cropping practised on paddy fields in Taiwan', *Joint Commission on Rural Reconstruction*.

CHOMBART DE LAUWE, J. B., and MORVAN, F. (1954), *Les possibilitiés de la petite entreprise dans l'agriculture française*, SADEPP.

CHRISTENSEN, R. P. (1966), 'Population growth and agricultural development', *Agricultural Economics Research*, vol. 18, pp. 119–28.

CHRISTENSEN, R. P. (1968), *Taiwan's Agricultural Development: Its Relevance for Developing Countries Today*, Foreign Agricultural Economic Report no. 39, US Department of Agriculture.

CHRISTENSEN, R. P. (1970), 'Problems and policies in the 1970s', *Economic Progress of Agriculture in Developing Nations 1950–68*, Foreign Agricultural Economic Report no. 59, US Department of Agriculture.

CHRISTODOULOU, D. (1966), 'Basic agrarian structural issues in the adjustment of African customary tenures to the needs of agricultural development', Food and Agricultural Organization, RU:WLR/66/C.

CLARK, R. J. (1968), 'Land reform and peasant market participation on the northern highlands of Bolivia', *Land Econ.*, vol. 44, pp. 153–72.

CLARK, R. J. (1970), 'Land reform in Bolivia', *Agency for International Development Spring Review of Land Reform*, vol. 6, pp. 1–96.

CLARK, R. J. (1971), 'Agrarian reform: Bolivia', in P. Dorner (ed.), *Land Reform in Latin America: Issues and Cases*, Land Economics Monograph no. 3.

COMITÉ INTERAMERICANO DE DESARROLLO AGRÍCOLA (1965), *Tenecia de la tierra y desarrollo socio-económico del sector agrícola*, Pan American Union.

COMMONS, J. R. (1957), *Legal Foundations of Capitalism*, University of Wisconsin Press.

CONRAD, A. H., and MEYER, J. R. (1964), *The Economics of Slavery and Other Studies in Econometric History*, Aldine. *Land Tenure Center Paper* no. 71, University of Wisconsin.

DALRYMPLE, D. G. (1969), *Imports and Plantings of High-Yielding Varieties of Wheat and Rice in the Less Developed Nations*, US Department of Agriculture, FEDR-8.

DALRYMPLE, D. G. (1971), *Survey of Multiple Cropping in Less Developed Nations*, US Department of Agriculture, FEDR-12.

DANDEKAR, V. M., and RATH, N. (1971), *Poverty in India*, Indian School of Political Economy.

DAVIS, L. H. (1970), 'United States assistance to agriculture in Latin America through the Agency for International Development',

DOMIKE, A. L. (1970), 'Colonization as an alternative to land reform', *Agency for International Development Spring Review of Land Reform*, vol. 11, pp. 1–19.

DORE, R. P. (1959), *Land Reform in Japan*, Oxford University Press.

DORNER, P. (1964), 'Land tenure, income distribution and productivity interactions', *Land Econ.*, vol. 40, pp. 247–54.

DORNER, P. (1966), 'Land tenure reform and agricultural development in Latin America', *Congressional Hearings*, US House of Reps., 89th US Congress, 2nd Sess.

DORNER, P. (1971a), 'Land tenure institutions', in M. G. Blase (ed.), *Institutions in Agricultural Development*, Iowa State University Press.

DORNER, P. (1971b), 'Needed redirections in economic analysis for agricultural development policy', *Amer J. of Agricul Econ.*, vol. 53, pp. 8–16.

DORNER, P. (1971c), 'Problems and policies of agricultural development: the United States experience', in R. Weitz (ed.), *Rural Development in a Changing World*, MIT Press.

DORNER, P., and FELSTEHAUSEN, H. (1970), 'Agrarian reform and employment: the Colombian case', *International Labour Review*, vol. 102, pp. 221–40.

DORNER, P., and KANEL, D. (1971), 'The economic case for land reform: employment, income distribution and productivity', *Land Reform: Land Settlement and Cooperatives*, FAO, ESR/Mono/71/1.

DORNER, P., THIESENHUSEN, W. C., and BROWN, M. (1965), 'The role of "feedback" in the formulation and implementation of development programs', *Land Tenure Center Newsletter* no. 19, University of Wisconsin.

DOVRING, F. (1962), 'Flexibility and security in agrarian reform programs', *Agrarian Reform and Economic Growth in Developing Countries*, US Department of Agriculture.

DOVRING, F. (1964), 'The share of agriculture in a growing population', in C. K. Eicher and L. W. Witt (eds), *Agriculture in Economic Development*, McGraw-Hill.

DOVRING, F. (1969), 'Land reform and productivity: the Mexican case', *Land Tenure Center Paper* no. 63, pp. 1–22.

DOVRING, F. (1970), 'Land reform in Mexico', *Agency for International Development Spring Review of Land Reform*, vol. 7, pp. 1–61.

ECKAUS, R. S. (1955), 'The factor proportions problem in underdeveloped areas', *Amer. Econ. Rev.*, vol. 45, pp. 539–65

ECKSTEIN, A. (1955), 'Land reform and economic development', *World Politics*, vol. 3, pp. 650–62.

ECKSTEIN, S. (1969), 'The macro-economic framework of the Mexican agrarian problem', *CIDA Paper* no. 11.

ECONOMIC COMMISSION FOR LATIN AMERICA (1964), *The Economic Development of Latin America in the Post-War Period*, United Nations, E/CN. 12/659/Rev. 1.

ECONOMIC COMMISSION FOR LATIN AMERICA (1968), 'Income distribution in Latin America', *Economic Bulletin for Latin America*, United Nations, vol. 12, no. 2, pp. 38–60.

EICHER, C., ZALLA, T., KOCHER, J., and WINCH, F. (1970), *Employment Generation in African Agriculture*, Institute of International Agriculture, Research Report no. 9, Michigan State University.

EL GHONEMY, M. R. (1968), 'Land reform and economic development in the Near East', *Land Econ.*, vol. 44. pp. 36–49.

FALCON, W. P. (1970), 'The green revolution: generations of problems', *Amer. J. of Agricul. Econ.*, vol. 52, pp. 698–710.

FEDERAL INSTITUTE FOR STATISTICS (1970), *Statistical Pocket Book of Yugoslavia*.

FELSTEHAUSEN, H. (1971), 'Agrarian reform: Colombia', in P. Dorner (ed.), *Land Reform in Latin America: Issues and Cases*, Land Economics Monograph no. 3.

FLORES, E. (1971), 'Rural development in Mexico', in R. Weitz (ed.), *Rural Development in a Changing World*, MIT Press.

FAO (1963), *Implementation of Price Stabilization Policies*.

FAO (1968), *The State of Food and Agriculture 1968*.

FAO (1970), *Agrarian Reform in Asia and the Far East*.

FAO (1971), *Report by the Special Committee on Agrarian Reform*.

FOSTER, P. (1970), 'Land reform in Algeria', *Agency for International Development Spring Review of Land Reform*, vol. 8, pp. 1–81.

GAITSKELL, A. (1971), 'The development of the Gezira in the Sudan', in R. Weitz (ed.), *Rural Development in a Changing World*, MIT Press.

GALBRAITH, J. K. (1951), 'Conditions for economic change in under-developed countries', *J. of Farm Econ.*, vol. 33, pp. 689–96.

GALBRAITH, J. K. (1967), *The New Industrial State*, Houghton-Mifflin.

GAYOSO, A. (1970), 'Land reform in Cuba', *Agency for International Development Spring Review of Land Reform*, vol. 7, pp. 1–95.

GREEN, R. H. (1970), 'The international economic system and development: some limitations of a special case', Economic Research Bureau Paper no. 70.4, University College, Dar es Salaam.

GRIFFIN, K. B. (1965), 'Algerian agriculture in transition', *Bull. of the Oxford University Inst of Eco and Stat*, vol. 27, pp. 232–5.

HANEY, E. (1969), 'The economic reorganization of minifundia in a highland community of Colombia', Ph.D. dissertation, University of Wisconsin.

HAVENS, A. E., and FLINN, W. F. (1970), *Internal Colonialism and Structural Change in Colombia*, Praeger.

HAYAMI, Y., and RUTTAN, V. W. (1970), 'Korean rice, Taiwan rice, and Japanese agricultural stagnation: an economic consequence of colonialism', *The Q. J. of Econ.*, vol. 84, pp. 562–89.

HERZ, B. K. (1970), 'Land reform in Kenya', *Agency for International Development Spring Review of Land Reform*, vol. 9, pp. 1–69.

JACOBY, E. H., with JACOBY, C. F. (1971), *Man and Land: The Fundamental Issue in Development*, André Deutsch.

JOHNSON, R. G., and BUSE, R. C. (1967), *A Study of Farm Size and Economic Performance in Old Santa Rosa, Rio Grande do Sul*, Land Tenure Center Research Paper no. 27, pp. 1–77.

JOHNSON, V. (1963), 'Lack of organization: Nigeria's main land tenure problem', *Land Tenure Center Newsletter* no. 7, University of Wisconsin.

JOHNSTON, B. F. (1970), 'Agriculture and structural transformation in developing countries: a survey of research', *J. of Economic Literature*, vol. 8, pp. 369–404.

JOHNSTON, B. F., and MELLOR, J. W. (1961), 'The role of agriculture in economic development', *Amer. Econ. Rev.*, vol. 51, pp. 566–93.

JOHNSTON, B. F., and COWNIE, J. (1969), 'The seed-fertilizer revolution and labor force absorption', *Amer. Econ. Rev.*, vol. 59, pp. 569–82.

KALDOR, N. (1959), 'Economic problems of Chile', *Economic Commission for Latin America*.

KANEL, D. (1967), 'Size of farm and economic development', *Indian J. of Agricul. Econ.*, vol. 22, pp. 26–44.

KANEL, D. (1971), 'Land tenure reform as a policy issue in modernization of traditional societies', in P. Dorner (ed.), *Land Reform in Latin America, Issues and Cases*, Land Economics Monograph no. 3.

KARST, K. L. (1964), 'Latin American land reform: the uses of confiscation', *Michigan Law Rev.*, vol. 63, pp. 327–72.

KAUTSKY, J. H. (ed.) (1962), *Political Change in Underdeveloped Countries: Nationalism and Communism*, Wiley.

KOO, A. Y. C. (1968), *The Role of Land Reform in Economic Development: A Case Study of Taiwan*, Praeger.

KOO, A. Y. C. (1970), 'Land reform in Taiwan', *Agency for International Development Spring Review of Land Reform*, vol. 3, pp. 1–70.

KOONE, H. D., and GLEECK, L. E. (1970), 'Land reform in the Philippines', *Agency for International Development Spring Review of Land Reform*, vol. 4, pp. 1–93.

LADEJINSKY, W. (1970), 'Ironies of India's green revolution', *Foreign Affairs*, vol. 38, pp. 758–68.

LEE, T. H. (1967), 'Intersectoral capital transfer in the economic development of Taiwan: a case study', Ph.D. dissertation, Cornell University.

LEE, T. H. (1968), 'Statistical tables, methodology, data sources and conclusions regarding intersectoral capital flows in the economic development of Taiwan, 1895–1960', Occasional Paper 11, Cornell University.

LIPSKI, W. (1969), *Agriculture in Poland*, Interpress Publishers.

LONG, E. J. (1952), 'Some theoretical issues in economic development', *J. of Farm Econ.*, vol. 34, pp. 723–33.

LONG, E. J. (1961), 'The economic basis of land reform in underdeveloped economies', *Land Econ.*, vol. 37, pp. 113–23.

LONG, E. J. (1962), 'The family farm in foreign land tenure policy', *J. of Farm Econ.*, vol. 44, pp. 536–49.

LONG, E. J. (1964), 'Institutional factors limiting progress in the less developed countries', in A. H. Moseman (ed.), *Agricultural Sciences for the Developing Nations*, Publication no. 76 of the American Association for the Advancement of Science.

MAREI, S. A. (1969), 'Overturning the pyramid,' *CERES*, vol 2, pp. 48–51.

MEEK, C. K. (1947), *Land Law and Custom in the Colonies*, Oxford University Press.

MELLOR, J. W. (1966), 'Toward a theory of agricultural development', in H. M. Southworth and B. F. Johnston (eds.), *Agricultural Development and Economic Growth*, Cornell University Press.

MELLOR, J. W. (1970), 'Review of *Agriculture and Economic Development: Symposium on Japan's Experience'*, by K. Ohkawa, B. F. Johnston and H. Kaneda (eds), *The Econ. Rev.*, vol. 21, no. 2.

MEYER, R. L. (1970), 'Debt repayment capacity of the Chilean agrarian reform beneficiaries', Ph.D. dissertation, Cornell University.

MILLIKAN, M. F. and HAPGOOD, D. (1967), *No Easy Harvest*, MIT Press.

MOORE, B. (1966), *Social Origins of Dictatorship and Democracy*, Beacon Press.

MORALES, H. (1964), 'Productividad presente y potencial en 96 predios de la Provincia de O'Higgins y su relación con el tamaño de las propiedades', memoria, Universidad de Chile.

MOSHER, A. T. (1969), *Creating a Progressive Rural Structure*, Agricultural Development Council, Inc.

MYRDAL, G. (1965), 'The United Nations, agriculture and world economic revolution', *J. of Farm Econ.*, vol. 47, pp. 889–99.

NICHOLLS, W. H. (1960), *Southern Tradition and Regional Progress*, University of North Carolina Press.

NICHOLLS, W. H. (1964), 'The place of agriculture in economic development', in C. K. Eicher and L. W. Witt (eds), *Agriculture in Economic Development*, McGraw-Hill.

NOVE, A. (1971), 'The decision to collectivize', in W. A. D. Jackson, (ed.), *Agrarian Policies and Problems in Communist and Non-Communist Countries*, University of Washington Press.

OWEN, W. F. (1966), 'The double developmental squeeze on agriculture', *Amer. Econ. Rev.*, vol. 56, pp. 43–70.

PARSONS, K. H. (1957), 'Land reform in the postwar era', *Land Econ.*, vol. 33, pp. 213–27.

PARSONS, K. H. (1962), 'Agrarian reform policy as a field of research' in *Agrarian Reform and Economic Growth in Developing Countries*, US Department of Agriculture.

PARSONS, K. H. (1971), 'Customary land tenure and the development of African agriculture', *Land Tenure Center Paper* no. 77, University of Wisconsin.

PARSONS, K. H., PENN, R. J. and RAUP, P. M. (1956), *Land Tenure: Proceedings of the International Conference on Land Tenure and Related Problems*, University of Wisconsin Press.

PENN, R. J. (1961), 'Public interest in private property (land)', *Land Econ.*, vol. 37, no. 2, pp. 99–104.

PLATT, K. B. (1970), 'Land reform in the United Arab Republic', *Agency for International Development Spring Review of Land Reform*, vol. 8, pp. 1–68.

POWELL, J. D. (1971), *Political Mobilization of the Venezuelan Peasant*, Harvard University Press.

PRESIDENT'S NATIONAL ADVISORY COMMISSION ON RURAL POVERTY (1967), *The People Left Behind*, US Government Printing Office.

QUIROS, R. (1971), 'Agricultural development and economic integration in Central America', Ph.D. dissertation, University of Wisconsin.

RAUP, P. M. (1960), 'Land tenure adjustments in industrial-agricultural economies', in *Modern Land Policy*, Papers of the Land Economics Institute, University of Illinois Press.

RAUP, P. M. (1967), 'Land reform and agricultural development', in H. M. Southworth and B. F. Johnston (eds.), *Agricultural. Development and Economic Growth*, Cornell University Press.

REYNOLDS, L. G. (1969), 'The contents of development economics', *Amer. Econ. Rev.*, vol. 59, pp. 401–8.

RUTTAN, V. W. (1966), 'Tenure and productivity of Philippine rice producing farms', *Philippines Econ. J.*, vol. 5, pp. 42–63.

RUTTAN, V. W. (1968), 'Production economics for agricultural development', *Indian J. of Agricul. Econ.s*, vol.23, pp. 1–14.

SALAS, O., KNIGHT, F. and SAENZ, C. (1970), *Land Titling in Costa Rica: A Legal and Economic Survey*, University of Costa Rica.

SCHAUB, J. R. (1970), 'Agriculture's performance in the developing countries', *Economic Progress of Agriculture in Developing Nations, 1950–1968*, US Department of Agriculture, Foreign Agricultural Economic Report no. 59.

SCHILLER, O. (1971), 'The communist experiences in dealing with the agrarian question: their significance for developing countries', in W. A. D. Jackson (ed.), *Agrarian Policies and Problems in Communist and Non-Communist Countries*, University of Washington Press.

SCHMID, L. (1967), 'The role of migratory labor in the economic development of Guatemala', *Land Tenure Center Research Paper* no. 22, University of Wisconsin.

SCHMID, L. (1969), 'Relation of size of farm to productivity', *Land Tenure Center Annual Report 1968*, University of Wisconsin.

SCHUMACHER, E. F. (1966), 'Economic development and poverty', *Intermediate Technology Development Group, Ltd.*, Bulletin no. 1, pp. 3–9.

SCHUMPETER, J. A. (1950), *Capitalism, Socialism and Democracy*, 3rd edn, Harper.

SEERS, D. (1969), 'The meaning of development', *International Develop. Rev.*, vol. 11, pp. 2–6.

SKRUBBELTRANG, F. (1953), *Agricultural Development and Rural Reform in Denmark*, FAO.

STERNBERG, M. J. (1971), 'Agrarian reform and employment, with special reference to Latin America', in *Agrarian Reform and Employment*, International Labour Office.

STEVENS, R. D. (1965), 'Role of growth in food requirements during economic development', *J. of Farm Econ.*, vol. 47, no. 5, pp. 1208–12.

THIESENHUSEN, W. C. (1966a), 'Chilean agrarian reform: the possibility of gradualistic turnover of land', *Inter-American Economic Affairs*, vol. 20, pp. 3–22.

THIESENHUSEN, W. C. (1966b), *Chile's Experiments in Agrarian Reform*, Land Economics Monograph no. 1, University of Wisconsin Press.

THIESENHUSEN, W. C. (1969), 'Population growth and agricultural employment in Latin America, with some US comparisons', *American Journal of Agricultural Economics*, vol. 51, pp. 735–52.

THIESENHUSEN, W. C. (1970), 'A suggested policy for industrial reinvigoration in Latin America', *Land Tenure Center Paper* no. 72, pp. 1–36.

THIESENHUSEN, W. C. (1971a), 'Agrarian reform: Chile', in P. Dorner (ed.), *Land Reform in Latin America: Issues and Cases*, Land Economics Monograph no. 3.

THIESENHUSEN, W. C. (1971b), 'Colonization: alternative or supplement to agrarian reform in Latin America', in P. Dorner (ed.), *Land Reform in Latin America: Issues and Cases*, Land Economics Monograph no. 3.

THOME, J. R. (1971a), 'Expropriation in Chile under the Frei agrarian reform', *Amer. J. of Comparative Law*, vol. 19, pp. 489–513.

THOME, J. R. (1971b), 'Improving land tenure security', in P. Dorner (ed.), *Land Reform in Latin America: Issues and Cases*, Land Economics Monograph no. 3.

TODARO, M. P. (1969), 'A model of labor migration and urban unemployment in less developed countries', *Amer. Econ. Rev.*, vol. 59, pp. 138–48.

TOSTLEBE, A. S. (1957), *Capital in Agriculture: Its Formation and Financing Since 1870*, Princeton University Press.

TREAKLE, H. C. (1970), 'Land reform in Iraq', *Agency for International Development Spring Review of Land Reform*, vol. 2, pp. 1–68.

UNITED NATIONS (1970), *Progress in Land Reform – Fifth Report*.

US DEPARTMENT OF AGRICULTURE (1963a), *Agriculture and Economic Growth*, Agricultural Economic Report no. 28.

US DEPARTMENT OF AGRICULTURE (1963b), *Indices of Agricultural Production for the twenty Latin American Countries*, Foreign Agricultural Economic Report no. 44.

US DEPARTMENT OF AGRICULTURE (1965), *Changes in Agriculture in twenty-six Developing Nations, 1948–1963*, Foreign Agricultural Economic Report no. 27.

US DEPARTMENT OF AGRICULTURE (1970), *Economic Progress of Agriculture in Developing Nations, 1950–68*, Foreign Agricultural Economic Report no. 59.

VOELKNER, H. E. (1970), 'Land reform in Japan', *Agency for International Development Spring Review of Land Reform*, vol. 3, pp. 1–79.

WALKER, K. R. (1965), *Planning in Chinese Agriculture*, Aldine.

WARRINER, D. (1955), *Land Reform and Economic Development*, National Bank of Egypt.

WARRINER, D. (1969), *Land Reform in Principle and Practice*, Oxford University Press.

WARRINER, D. (1970), 'Employment and income aspects of recent agrarian reforms in the Middle East', *International Labour Rev.*, vol. 101, pp. 605–25.

WHARTON, C. R. (1969), 'The green revolution: cornucopia or Pandora's box?', *Foreign Affairs*, vol. 47, pp. 464–76.

WILKENING, E. A. and IUTAKA, S. (1967), 'Sociological aspects of colonization as viewed from Brazil', *Land Tenure Center Paper*, no. 37, University of Wisconsin.

WING, H. E., Jr (1970), 'Land reform in Venezuela', *Agency for International Development Spring Review of Land Reform*, vol. 5, pp. 1–68.

Index